Heart of the Warrior
Learning the Combat Skills of King David

Heart of the Warrior
Learning the Combat Skills of King David

By Genesis Pilgrim

This is the path: Be filled with supernatural power. Become a spiritual warrior.

Table of Contents

1 … Agility and Elusiveness
2 … Anger
5 … Camp & Defense Locations
10 … Celebration
11 … Compliments, Popularity & Honors
15 … Conscience & Emotions
17 … Country
18 … Courage & Bravery
22 … Criticism
26 … Cross-Training, Leave & Rest
29 … Crying
31 … Cut Off Enemy Supplies & Ambush His Re-Supply
33 … Deception
36 … Decisions and Advisers
37 … Deterring Enemy Attacks
40 … Discipline & Confrontation
44 … Distrust & Trust
51 … Encryption, Coded Communication & Whispering
54 … Extra Duties
56 … Faith & Proof of God
59 … Family
62 … Fear
64 … Ferocity
66 … Flanking Attack
68 … Follow-on Attacks
69 … Food
71 … Funerals & Grieving

72 ... Garrisons

74 ... Gear

75 ... God Fights for David

83 ... God's Will

86 ... Grief & Mourning

88 ... History, Heritage & Tradition

90 ... Hope

92 ... Influencing Others

94 ... Insults & Dissent

98 ... Jobs You Don't Want

100 ... Labor & Officials

102 ... Leadership from the Front

108 ... Lies, Manipulation & Slander

114 ... Mental Clarity & Prayer

115 ... Mentorship & Professional Development

120 ... Mercy & Compassion

123 ... Messengers & Couriers

126 ... Motivation & Inspiration

129 ... Music & Dancing

131 ... Name & Legacy

133 ... No Witnesses

134 ... Opportunist

138 ... Organization in Thirds & Mutual Support

144 ... Peaceful Resolution (if possible)

145 ... Perception & Walking by Faith (2 Cor. 5:7)

148 ... Physical Endurance & Mental Resilience

150 ... Planning & Advisers

153 ... Plots & Betrayal

156 ... Plunder

158 ... Poise

159 ... Predict Human Behavior

166 ... Pride & Desired Outcome

168 ... Promises & Pledges

171 ... Promotions & Billets

174 ... Prophetic Leaders & Advisers

180 ... Quickness & Holy Spirit Indwelling

185 ... Raids

186 ... Rally Points & Contingency Plans

188 ... Read Books

190 ... Readiness

192 ... Reforming Troops

194 ... Religion

213 ... Repentance & Paying Amends

214 ... Reserves

218 ... Siege

220 ... Simplicity & Homesickness

223 ... Situational Awareness, Scouts & Informants

227 ... Stealth & Concealment

232 ... Subordinate Leaders

235 ... Supernatural Power

236 ... Supplies & Resources

239 ... Tact, Humility & Professionalism

244 ... Teamwork & Allies

249 ... Terror

253 ... Tribute Payments

254 ... Trust & Confidence

256 ... Vigilance & Wariness

258 ... Violence & Intensity

262 ... War-Gaming, Contingencies & Back-up Plans
264 ... Warrior
265 ... Watchmen
266 ... Weapon Proficiency
267 ... Wills & Dying Wishes
268 ... Women

<u>Introduction</u>

During my time in the U.S. Marines, I read many inspirational books on warfare. Some of my favorite include, <u>Rifleman Dodd</u> by C.S. Forester, and the ancient book, <u>The Art of War</u> by Sun Tzu. There are many others—and largely I owe my military success to the many authors who inspired me with their work.

In turn, being a warrior who has stepped away from the battlefields of my past, I want to make a personal contribution to future warriors. So, here I debut my work on King David—the immortal, supernatural warrior.

There is much a warrior can learn from David. Perhaps the most prominent lesson is found within David's ability to use the vision and imagination of his mind as a source of incredible power. In my assessment, throughout David's life he had no "culminating point."

His spirituality was so powerful he always had more to draw from within—enabling him to fight well beyond the limits of merely physical men. In my first book, <u>Dear David: Learning to See God through PTSD, Anxiety and Depression</u>, I trace the development of David's spiritual abilities to his PTSD. Psychologically we can evaluate David's mind through his many psalms—allowing us to see exactly why and how he became capable of gaining such power.

Beyond basic physical skills (running, firing a rifle, etc.), I am convinced "faith" as a firmly held conviction is the most decisive characteristic of any warrior. Faith inspires confidence, courage and commitment. Faith gives a person the courage to step onto the battlefield. Then faith keeps him there by giving a "second wind" ability to persevere in hardship.

A person who simply thinks of himself may be inclined to give up. But a person who is "faithful" to his fellow warriors will push himself well beyond his physical limits for the sake of his nation and his people. Thus, faith inspires the individual to continue no matter the hardship.

David's faith in God provided him with a bottomless well of courage and strength. As a *physical* warrior, David was *intimidating*—having the ability to use weapons with skill and precision. However, as a *spiritual* warrior, David was absolutely *immortal*—having the ability to draw endlessly from a supernatural fortress of power he saw around and above him.

Do you desire this power?

Read further . . .

Heart of the Warrior

Genesis Pilgrim

How to Use this Book

This book is designed in devotional format. It has no chapters.

Simply find a topic listed in the "Table of Contents." Flip to that page. Read and reflect. Then return to read another paragraph or two when you have time.

Read and apply lessons contained herein— one paragraph at a time. Don't overwhelm yourself, but work on developing different skills discussed in this book over time.

How do you eat an elephant?

One bite at a time.

Do not feel as if you need to read this book from cover to cover.

Author's Reflection

Dear Reader,

This book is intended to be used for quick reference, so some information is duplicated under different section titles.

But in those cases where you find something repeated, think about it this way . . .

Maybe I am repeating it because I really want to make sure you "get it." And, since I can't stomp my foot to clue you to something important, I must use other devices—such as repeating myself.

Also, Bible passages usually contain several memorable lessons, so it makes sense for me to comment on Bible passages *multiple* times.

In other words, read this book *SLOWLY.* If you are getting déjà vu, then you are reading too fast! Slow down. Read one paragraph, work on it for a week, then read another paragraph next week.

There is no point powering through this book: Work through it slowly during your entire time in the military.

Anyway, I hope you enjoy my book.

Stay safe.

No matter what, come home to us.

Fair Winds and Following Seas,
In Christ,

Genesis Pilgrim

<u>Agility & Elusiveness</u>

Practice being quick on your feet . . .

There are many ways to develop agility. Basically any sport will help you gain physical quickness. So, play sports. Run. Lift weights. All these activities may help you to gain physical skill which may one day save your life.

So, how did David develop agility? . . .

Dancing.

In 2 Samuel 6:5, 12-14, David joins in the musical celebration during the movement of the ark. David's dancing ability was doubtlessly a part of his physical agility. Therefore, David's musical ability, in an unlikely fashion, also enhanced his battlefield performance.

When engaged in combat, David would have had the agility to dance around his opponent. This is revealed in his ability to dodge Saul's spears.

In 1 Samuel 18:10-11, David dodges two spears thrown by King Saul.

A similar occurrence is found in 1 Samuel 19:10.

Later in 1 Samuel 20:33, King Saul throws a spear at his son, Jonathan, and misses.

Find a sport you enjoy. Take care to develop physical agility.

<u>Anger</u>

Having a dominating presence as a military leader can save the lives of your people. A leader who appears intimidating and powerful to outsiders may dissuade would-be attackers from attempting to fight that leader's unit. In other words, the leader wants to make his group appear absolutely ferocious to all outsiders. In dangerous situations, you never know who may be sizing you up from a distance.

A leader's intensity causes others in his unit to respond a certain way. A good leader considers the effects of his actions on others. So, in some cases it is good for military leaders to even fake anger just to motivate subordinates to try harder.

In a similar way, David used anger in his military leadership to gain certain responses from others.

For example, in 2 Samuel 11:18-20, Joab expects David to have an angry outburst upon receiving a certain battle report. In this case the expression of anger is memorable to subordinates and continues to guide their behavior even in the leader's absence. In this way, anger is a tool used by the leader to inspire and motivate subordinates to particular actions.

Controlled anger vs. uncontrolled anger . . .

If someone is an effective leader, anger is a controlled emotion. It is used in a psychological fashion to provide an enduring positive/negative reinforcement loop within the minds of subordinates.

Anger can also be used by a leader to compel or manipulate a certain response from another.

For example, in 1 Samuel 25, when David heard a man named Nabal insulted him, David responded angrily. He stated he would fight and kill all of Nabal's men.

Of course, David did not go through with his threat—however, his intense response may have somehow inspired the reaction of Abigail, who later arrived with a gift to dissuade David. So, it is interesting to consider if David simply used his anger as a well-placed tool of persuasion—compelling others to predictable actions which would be favorable to him.

In other words, David may have never intended to fight and kill Nabal's men. But by making them think he was angry enough to kill them, it compelled Abigail to bring the gift of food. Thus, the well-placed use of anger as a tool of persuasion accomplished David's original purpose: getting food for his army.

Uncontrolled anger . . .

In other cases, David has angry outbursts which do not seem to be controlled. These outbursts were likely a symptom of his PTSD . . .

For example, in 2 Samuel 12:5, David has an angry outburst when having a discussion with the prophet Nathan. When David was told a man stole and killed another man's sheep, he immediately stated the accused should be put to death. This demonstrates David had anger which overrode his other senses—prescribing a death penalty based on hearsay without granting the accused opportunity to face his accusers nor answer for himself.

Also, in 2 Samuel 6:8, David was angry at the death of the priest, Uzzah. In this case, Uzzah died for an irreverent, preventable death due to a mistake in carrying the ark improperly. David was likely angry with several people—Uzzah for messing up, the priests for not knowing the proper procedure, and himself for failing to properly oversee the priests.

Sometimes we just feel angry. Although *controlled anger* can be productive and necessary; *uncontrolled anger* may cloud our minds in a negative way. When leading others, consider how your anger will be perceived by outsiders and your subordinates. Then use anger in a controlled fashion to gain a desired psychological response. Don't allow your anger to be uncontrolled.

<u>Camp & Defense Locations</u>

Basic principles for setting up a camp

Be ready and able to move out quickly . . .

In 1 Samuel 23:13-14 it says David's army kept moving to different places to confuse Saul.[1] In the military this concept is captured by the oft repeated phrase, "shoot—move—communicate." When forward deployed a military unit should always be doing one of the three activities. It is more difficult for an enemy to hit a moving target than a stationary one. Don't be a sitting duck.

Pick defendable spots for camping . . .

When staying in a certain location, pick a spot which is defendable.

When moving to a location where you intend to stay it may be necessary to send a "quartering party" ahead of your main force. This allows your unit to recon the area with just a couple vehicles before the rest of the vehicles arrive. Upon arrival of the main force, the quartering party can direct the remaining vehicles.

Upon arrival, a watch schedule needs to be set to ensure there are always people looking out for approaching enemies. A hasty defensive position

---

[1] 1 Sam. 22:5; 23:29; 25:1; 26:2-3; 2 Sam. 1-2

should be established, with weapons oriented toward an enemy's most likely avenue of approach. There should also be a plan on what your people will do in different scenarios.

Setting up a camp headquarters . . .

At times it may become necessary to set up a headquarters location. From the headquarters location leaders can coordinate efforts of all assigned units—usually through plotting last reported locations of each, scheduling resupply for those units, providing an initial location for medical evacuation (MEDEVAC) and so on.

In 2 Samuel 17:24, David makes Mahanaim the headquarters for his army during Absalom's rebellion. Interestingly, Mahanaim is the location where the patriarch, Jacob, saw a spectacular vision of angels—who were sent to protect him during his treacherous journey to meet with his brother, Esau (Gen. 32:1-2). In this way, the story of David somewhat mirrors the experience of Jacob. Whereas God showed Jacob the "glory" of angels sent to protect him; God sent a man, named Shobi, which means "glory" to provide David's army with bedding, bowls, pottery, wheat, barley, flour, grain, beans, honey, curds, sheep and cheese (2 Sam. 17:28-29).

Other camp issues . . .

Safety is always a priority. One of the most critical safety issues is making sure all vehicles are ground-guided. This means all vehicles driving in an area have a person walking ahead of them. This ensures vehicles will not roll over areas where people may be laying on the ground asleep.

For camping scenarios where there is no risk of enemy contact, lesser matters are considered—such as marking off locations where people can brush their teeth, urinate and so on.

Stay in the wilderness rather than preexisting buildings . . .

Sometimes you may be able to use a preexisting settlement as a camping location. However, in these locations be wary of traps and mines—particularly in doorways of houses. Perhaps when considering the high likelihood of traps which may be present in preexisting structures, it might be more prudent to keep your unit out of buildings which could have been tampered with by your enemy.

In the Bible, David sought protection for his family within the Moab stronghold (1 Sam. 22:3-4). But, later the prophet warned him to leave this area—most likely to avoid a trap of some kind (1 Sam. 22:5). So, David preferred rather to use natural fortresses in the wilderness—taking advantage of caves and rock formations in the hills.

Later, in 2 Samuel 5:9, David establishes Zion as his royal fortress in Jerusalem. Although he takes measures to build up Zion's defenses, we see in the Psalms David always felt anxiety within his castle. Even though David lived behind grand walls, he constantly suspected those in his court as plotting against him.

Why?

The warrior who survives develops hypervigilance around people who *could* be enemies. This is why David felt at peace in the wilderness but in the city he felt anxiety.

Perhaps in your military travels it would be wise to put this teaching from David into practice. Avoid camping within preexisting settlements at all costs. Try to remain in the wilderness—where you have a far greater likelihood of evading traps.

The spiritual fortress . . .

Most notably, David viewed God's presence as a supernatural stronghold—which would protect him constantly (Psa. 2:12; 5:11; 7:1; 8:2; 9:9; 11:1; 14:6; 16:1; 17:7; 18:2, 30-31, 46; 19:14; 25:20; 27:1, 5; 28:1, 8; 31:1-4, 19-20; 34:8, 22; 36:7; 37:39-40; 40:2; 52:7; 55:8; 57:1; 59:1, 9, 16-17; 61:2-4; 62:2, 6-8; 64:10; 95:1; 141:8; 142:4-5; 144:1-2).

David indeed was at emotional peace when in the wilderness without walls around him. In those isolated places, far from others, with his army with him, David felt far safer than he did within his Zion fortress—or any other physical fortress for that matter.

A perfect example of this is found within Psalm 23—where David shares his abiding sense of peacefulness experienced in the wilderness.

No matter where you may find yourself, think of God as your supernatural fortress—travelling above you like a grand machine in the sky. God will never abandon you—so even if you are stuck in a difficult place, you can be sure God will somehow grant you the ability to persevere.

<u>Celebration</u>

In 2 Samuel 6:20-22, David was loved by the people who joined with him in joyful celebration before the Lord. Although he was criticized for his lack of royal bearing, David preferred instead to please the Lord rather than those who criticized him.

If you are a leader, set up morale events for your troops to celebrate. When I served in the Marines, I would set up Mess Nights for my troops. Morale events build camaraderie and have the effect of making those you lead esteem you more highly. Especially if you are hard on your troops, you will need morale events to balance your heavy hand as a demanding leader.

When appropriate celebrate with your troops. But do so with restraint, having in place plans to ensure no one is driving drunk or doing anything illegal. Although you may choose to abstain from drinking alcohol, your troops might drink. A good leader puts plans in place to protect their troops who drink—ensuring they do not make bad decisions. Assign drivers before you begin events and have leaders situated near the doors to ensure everyone is following the driving plan precisely.

Compliments, Popularity & Honors

In the military, sometimes people will like you and sometimes they will not.

Why?

Who knows? People can be fickle.

However, when you are praised, receive it in humility. Perhaps you should consider underestimating yourself. Pride goes before a fall. And, if you feel as if the compliment serves no other purpose than to personally puff you up, don't let it set you up for failure.

A common way to redirect praises as a leader would be to praise the other warriors in your unit. From time to time when leaders are awarded medals, you may hear them saying their accomplishments were really "team accomplishments"—and they are wearing the medal in honor of their team. This is a good practice.

Love is a complicated emotion—where stakes are high. On one hand, if a person is loved, they are cared for dearly by another. But, as is often the case, if the love is somehow broken, the one who loves will be stirred to intense hatred.

For example, consider a relationship which ends badly. Indeed if the couple did not begin a relationship with one another they would likely still be cordial as dear friends. But "love lost" often brings on intense dislike—so much so it would have been better to have avoided love in the first place.

Need proof?

In 1 Samuel 16:21-22 it states David was initially liked by King Saul. However, the king later became jealous of David's battlefield ability and sought to kill him.

In 1 Samuel 18:5 it states the army officers and troops were all pleased with David being awarded a high rank in the military. But later David was betrayed by many of these people and compelled to flee the country.

In 2 Samuel 19:9-15, after Absalom's rebellion was stopped, the people of Israel and Judah desired to welcome David back from his army camp in Mahanaim—asking him to resume his kingship.

David was so loved by the people that Israel and Judah disputed over who had a closer allegiance to David (2 Sam. 19:40-43). Yet the love of Israel was shallow indeed because they immediately rebelled against David to follow Sheba, son of Bikri (2 Sam. 20:1).

If you want to be "liked" in the military, be proficient. In 1 Samuel 18:16 it says all Israel and Judah loved David due to his faithful military leadership. By focusing on doing a good job in the military, David gained the favor of all the people.

In 1 Samuel 18:30, it states David became more famous than the other commanders due to his leadership success on battlefields.

This is a good thing about the military—as long as one does a good job, they can gain favor with many. In the military, popularity is simply based on proficiency; not arbitrary whims as in other areas of society. There are exceptions to this, but generally speaking if you do a good job in the military, you will gain favor with others. Although you may suffer betrayal and other bad things from those who are jealous, the general fact is if you focus on doing a good job, people will like you.

Honor—Pass it on to others

In 2 Samuel 2:4, David was entreated by the elders of Judah to serve as their king. Thus, David did not fight or presume kingship upon himself. The people asked him to rule over them.

Later, in 2 Samuel 5:2, the leaders of Israel acknowledge David's leadership similar to the Judges of old. It is this recognition which prompts the elders of Israel to ask David to serve as their king as well. In this way, David unites the kingdoms of Judah and Israel.

In all cases, when you are honored find a way to use it to benefit others. Share good things with your countrymen. Pass on blessings and compliments to others—allowing them to join with you in your exaltation. The moment in which you are honored will shortly pass. So, while you have opportunity in the spotlight, use it to praise others in your team. By doing this you can take full advantage of your opportunity and make a long-lasting positive benefit emerge from your brief time of exaltation.

Last, in 2 Samuel 3:36-37, the people approved of David's actions at the funeral of Abner, the general of Israel. As a leader, be mindful of times where you should show honor in a special way for your troops. Award your troops. Honor their memory and make them a part of your unit's legacy.

Conscience & Emotions

Your conscience to speaks to you . . .

As a warrior, allow your conscience to direct you. Never lose connection with your conscience.

Trauma can damage one's conscience. In the aftermath of trauma, a person may develop PTSD—which can cause emotional spikes at random times. Thus, a person with PTSD may no longer sense a cause-effect relationship between "how they feel" and his surroundings. In other words, the emotions of a person with PTSD can become detached from his control.

Therefore, if you are a warrior who has been thus affected by past trauma, interact with your conscience often—even if what you are compelled to do goes against it. Stay in touch with how you feel, and why you feel as you do. This will ensure you do not lose touch with yourself as a result of battlefield experiences.

When you do something wrong, admit to it. At times these mistakes may seem small, but by owning your mistakes you can learn more about yourself and deepen your connection to your own emotions.

For example, David was conscience stricken after cutting off a corner of King Saul's robe (1 Sam. 24:5).

David also becomes conscience stricken after ordering an unnecessary census of Israel (2 Sam. 24:10).

Also, in repeated trauma, a warrior may feel compelled to set aside emotions like compassion in order to focus on his mission. A warrior cannot stop in the middle of a battlefield to grieve losses. So it is common for a warrior to continue fighting, pushing aside compassion and grief, in order to stay focused. But eventually one's mind wants to bring them back to those moments where they "should" have been permitted to grieve and mourn.

In the aftermath of battles you may feel detached from yourself—as if you are missing something. Let me encourage you to re-visit past battlefields with a counselor. Think deeply about moments where you wanted to show compassion and empathy and were not permitted to do so. By doing this you will reestablish and strength your connection to yourself.

During battles your first priority was survival. But after battles be sure to meet once again with your normal self—your conscience. Don't leave your conscience behind you. Allow your heart & conscience time to catch up with you—fully processing what happened. By doing so, you can grow stronger.

<u>Country</u>

In the book of Judges, God would raise up a leader, called a "judge," to deliver Israel from harm. Although the Judges all had faults, they were to be embraced by their nation. This same principle extends beyond the Judges. Even when threatened by Saul, David refused to harm him because he was the anointed leader of Israel (1 Sam. 24:6, 10; 26:9-11, 23). Harming the leader of Israel would result in the harming of the nation itself. So, anointed military leaders need to be protected until they fully completed their assigned God-given purpose (2 Sam. 21:17).

Likewise, a military man should love the country for which he fights—recognizing he has been raised up to defend his people. In 1 Samuel 26:19-20, David shows his love for the Lord's inheritance. Being driven away from his country was an affliction to his soul. David desires to return to his home country.

The calling of the warrior is to endure danger on behalf of his people. By faithfulness to duty a warrior removes harm from his citizens.

Courage & Bravery

How does a warrior become courageous?
The source of courage is supernatural.
Physical strength is physical. But, a spiritual warrior has the ability to fight beyond his normal physical abilities. When a person believes God is with him, he has the mental ability to confront any physical challenge—even death itself. This is clearly seen throughout the battle experiences of David, where he constantly looked to the Lord as his source of courage.

Courage means enduring danger for your people . . .
The bravery of the warrior is found in his continued willingness to endure danger for the sake of his people.

In 1 Samuel 16:18, David is described as brave—even before the boy has the opportunity to face Goliath in battle.

Later, in 1 Samuel 19:5, Jonathan says David "took his life in his hands" when he fought Goliath. This means David knew he "could" have died, yet his love for his people compelled him to take that risk.

Over time, David's courage was contagious—inspiring his subordinate soldiers to be likewise brave and valiant (2 Sam. 17:10).

Prayer gives courage and guidance . . .

David's prayers gave him courage and guidance. In 1 Samuel 23:2-4, David inquires of the Lord. God answers David—most likely through the mediation of the priest, Abiathar. This inner faith is the source of great courage and confidence. A person who believes God is directing his actions will become capable of greater feats. This faith in God is the source of David's battlefield ferocity.

In 2 Samuel 5:19-20, David prays and God directs him to attack the Philistine army at Baal Perazim. Following this battle, God gives David specific instructions on how to successfully attack the Philistines in the Valley of Rephaim (2 Sam. 5:22-24). These directions from God gave David courage to carry out the instructions.

In 1 Samuel 30:6-8, David was distressed when his soldiers wanted to stone him following the destruction of Ziklag by the Amalekites. David gains incredible courage and confidence in this situation by immediately calling for the priest and sacred ephod. In this brief time of prayer, David receives guidance from the Lord—directing him to pursue and destroy the Amalekite army.

Faith can make you a stronger fighter . . .

This is an interesting concept—which we fully acknowledge in any task requiring physical activity. We often hear it said that running, weight-lifting and every other imaginable physical exercise is *"more mental than physical."* We have heard it said, *"Where there is a will, there is a way."*

We all have normal physical limits. However if we believe we have a source of strength beyond our own muscles, then we are able to mentally push ourselves further and further. In this regard, spiritual faith is incredibly useful to the warrior because it allows him to fight harder than he would be otherwise capable.

So, a spiritual warrior can be a far more powerful opponent than a merely physical warrior. Consider how martial arts often intersect with spirituality—and within this merging you may find how spirituality can vastly enhance the battlefield abilities of the warrior.

In the Bible, David fought with supernatural power—being convinced God was fighting through him (2 Sam. 7:9). This made David incredibly courageous and confident on the battlefield. If you desire this power, the path is spiritual, not physical.

Your faith must be strong, not weak . . .

In 2 Samuel 7:22, we see David believed his God to be completely unique and more powerful than any other "gods." This exclusivity in his religious beliefs would have granted David additional courage and confidence on the battlefield. Whereas other men may have thought it possible for the gods of others to defeat their own god; David altogether rejected this thought. In David's mind, there is no other supernatural being who is a match for his own God. Thus, David wielded an incredible spiritual enhancement to his battlefield abilities. He believed himself invincible through his direct association with God. And, countless battlefields proved it to be so. David was never defeated.

Thus, the pathway of the spiritual warrior is time-tested and proven. If you desire to be a warrior, do not be merely physical. Adopt within yourself spirituality and thereby gain additional confidence and courage to help you in time of need. Develop the ability to see beyond the veil—importing power into our world through your body. Walk by faith, not by sight (2 Cor. 5:7).

Criticism

How to endure criticism . . .

No matter what, all leaders must endure criticism. Eventually, even the best leaders receive criticism from those who are bent on viewing them negatively. Below I will present some methods which may be used to help you navigate these difficult experiences when you face them . . .

Pray for mental clarity . . .

In 1 Samuel 18:9, King Saul begins viewing David with suspicion. Rather than buckling under pressure, David continually endures through prayer—as evidenced in his many psalms.

Unfortunately we may find ourselves the subject of others' hate. At times leaders in charge of you may be trying to use you as a scapegoat for their own incompetence. In these cases it might be impossible for us to change the other person's perception of us.

If you find yourself in a situation where it seems impossible—pray. Often we find if we seclude ourselves and meditate we can emerge from those moments of reflection with greater clarity—helping us to better confront the challenges we face. Even in the midst of many enemies who are bearing down upon you, God can give you peace—seating you before him as an honored guest in His spiritual banquet (Psa. 23:5).

This is exactly how David thought. In addition to praying, he also wrote psalms—where he vented his feelings about the hopelessness of his situations. So, perhaps you could also write down how you feel as a part of your prayers. This method may help you to cope with the difficulties within your situation.

Separate yourself from the problem . . .

In 2 Samuel 6:16, 20-23, David endures the criticism of his wife, Michal. She scorns David for his lack of kingly dignity in his dancing. David, however, challenges her criticism—claiming it was most proper for him to dance as a part of his worship before God.

In the above case, David separated himself from Michal. He didn't divorce her. He simply removed himself from her presence so he wouldn't be torn down all the time.

In some situations where you are experiencing criticism from a leader in the military, perhaps it makes the most sense to ask for orders to a new duty station. Rather than having to deal with problems every day, you could choose to take your receipt of criticism as a cue for the beginning of something new. If you are not stuck, do not allow yourself to feel stuck. Move to greener pastures.

Ignore harmless criticism . . .

In 2 Samuel 16:5-13, David overlooks the cursing of a Benjamite who walked next to David's group as he fled Absalom's rebellion. Rather than assenting to Abishai, one of his warriors who wanted to kill the Benjamite, David chose to leave the Benjamite alone. Instead, David hopes the curses of the Benjamite will inspire God's increased blessing on himself. David continued to walk as the Benjamite threw rocks and dirt at him (2 Sam. 16:13).

In some cases you will receive *harmless* criticism. In the above situation, David completely ignored the Benjamite who cursed him. At the end of the situation, David even muses about it (2 Sam. 19:22). Ultimately, the criticisms of the Benjamite did not change David's identity as the King of Israel and Judah.

So, if you receive criticism which does not affect you, truly bearing no ability to harm you— consider ignoring it. Laugh it off. If a subordinate mentions it to you, laugh about it with him. Your jovial dismissal of harmless criticism will actually make you look better to your subordinates.

Consider relieving or reassigning a critical subordinate . . .

In 2 Samuel 19:5-7, David's general, Joab, advantageously threatens David he will lead away the army from his kingship unless he stops grieving for the death of Absalom. David complies with Joab and stops grieving. He overlooks Joab's threat rather than immediately punishing him for it.

However, later when it made sense to do so, David relieved Joab of his command—giving Joab's job to Amasa (2 Sam. 19:13).

Always consider if you trust your subordinates. If a subordinate demonstrates they are not working with you in good faith, do not trust him further. At the next available opportunity, punish or reassign him elsewhere. Within your military unit you cannot afford to have saboteurs working under you. You cannot afford to have subordinate leaders who are secretly working against you. So, consider relieving or reassigning the person.

<u>Cross-Training, Leave & Rest</u>

All units should have depth on their roster. This allows others to step in while others rest. Then the leader can rotate warriors in and out of battle. This ensures those on the fighting lines are rested and mentally prepared—rather than just throwing one's entire unit in the fight—completely exhausting all the soldiers with no opportunity for respite.

So, how can you do this for your unit?

Train subordinates to take the place of one another and their leaders. Then give them opportunities to cross-train and be in charge in the absence of others. For example, if a troop asks you for leave, your immediate response should always be: *"Who will be in charge of what you do while you are gone?"* Then, before you allow the person to leave you should conduct a brief with both individuals to ensure the one covering duties is fully prepared for his extra duties.

Then you candidly tell the person taking leave if his replacement messes anything up you will recall him from leave. This will make the person going on leave have a vested interest in ensuring his replacement is the right person for the job. If this is practiced in times of peace, your unit will have the ability to persevere long-term in battle.

Cross-Training

Concerning cross-training, when you train subordinates to step into different billets it provides coverage in the case of battle losses. If anyone is hurt or wounded, there should be multiple warriors who are capable of covering down on the wounded person's normal duties.

In 2 Samuel 11:1, David trusts Joab to lead Israel's army. This is different from King Saul—who led expeditions personally. Thus, trusting in subordinate leaders allows a leader more flexibility—and in this case it allowed David to rest from warfare.

Indeed, when comparing Saul to David, we see this is a striking difference between these two leaders. Whereas Saul did not even have a champion to fight for him against Goliath; David had an entire court of "mighty men"—all of whom were valorous, proficient warriors capable of leading others (2 Sam. 23:8-39). David often led from the front during his military campaigns, but he also extended the honor of leadership to those men in his command who proved themselves capable in past battles. As a result, David's entire army was vastly superior to the army of Saul.

Take Care of your Body

In 2 Samuel 16:14, David and his company press on to reach their destination when fleeing from Absalom's rebellion. But, upon reaching their destination, David rests and restores himself.

Never forget to take care of your body. When you have opportunity to rest, post a guard and allow yourself to regain your strength.

In all ways, remember you are the shepherd of your own body. Feed it properly. Take care of it. Be mindful of yourself. And, as you do this you will be capable of fighting better.

<u>Crying</u>

Crying gives mental clarity and focus . . .

In 1 Samuel 30:4, David's home base of Ziklag was raided by the Amalekites. David and his army men cry until they can cry no longer.

Although it would seem right for the soldiers to hold their bearing, suppressing emotion as they sought to rescue their family members, instead the battle hardened warrior David cries—and encourages his men to do so.

Why?

Crying gives us the ability to process and let go of grief—giving us the ability to get through the rest of the day.

A warrior may be tempted to push aside the desire to cry when he experiences loss. However, if he allows those emotions to quickly flood to the surface, dealing with them in short order, it may allow his brain to re-focus on the task at hand.

Anyone who cries understands this. Sometimes, all you can do is cry. And, after you cry, your brain seems re-focused.

So, when you need to cry . . . Cry.

In some situations it might not be appropriate for you to cry in front of others—and in those situations excuse yourself so you can cry and re-focus yourself. Let go of those emotions. Although crying does not fix our problems, it provides mental clarity to help us get through the day.

There are many situations where David cried. . . .

In 2 Samuel 1:17-27, David mourns for Saul and Jonathan by reciting a funeral lament.

In 2 Samuel 3:31-39, David mourns and grieves at the funeral of Abner.

In 2 Samuel 12:22, David states he wept as he fasted for his sick, infant son.

In 2 Samuel 13:36-37, David weeps for many days after hearing his son, Absalom, murdered his son, Amnon.

In 2 Samuel 15:30-31, David wept, covered his head and walked barefoot as he fled from Absalom's rebellion.

Last, in 2 Samuel 18:33-19:4, David grieved and wept after hearing of the death of his son, Absalom.

The most powerful warriors, like David, find a way to use their body's biology to sharpen their battlefield performance. Without a doubt, crying can make a warrior more prepared for the next phase of battle. Cry to re-frame your perspective—providing a clear break from the past mission to your present mission. This will allow you to fully focus on your new task.

<u>Cut off Enemy Supplies &</u>
<u>Ambush His Re-Supply</u>

Cut off enemy supplies . . .

To fight wars, an army needs the three B's . . . Beans, Bullets and Band-Aids. So, if you ever need to defeat an enemy without firing a shot, simply take away those supplies.

One of the best military strategies is to cut off the supplies of an enemy army. This allows you to avoid battle while rapidly bringing an enemy to their culminating point—compelling surrender.

This can be done by destroying their re-supply route. Or it can be done by leading the enemy to become too far from their re-supply points. One example of this is found in World War 2—when the Russian army allowed the Nazi army to move further and further into the depth of Russia. Eventually, the Nazi army was so hopelessly dispersed within the cold Russian interior they were far beyond their own ability to provide for their army.

Always anticipate your enemy's next move . .
.

By denying your enemy supplies, you become capable of predicting their next actions. If an enemy needs fuel for their vehicles and food for their soldiers, then you can predict a re-supply train will be moving in their direction. So, if you are able to guess the re-supply route, it is a no-brainer to stage an ambush on that route to intercept the re-supply. By doing so, you not only seize the supplies which were intended for your enemy, but you make your enemy increasingly more desperate—and much more likely to surrender.

A similar technique is used by David in the Bible . . .

In 2 Samuel 8:4, David's army ambushes the forces of Hadadezer, king of Zobah, as they moved to solidify their control along the Euphrates River. It appears this army included a supply caravan—due to the large numbers of horses and chariots.

Then, David's army set an ambush for the next group of Arameans (2 Sam. 8:5). David's army ambushed the Arameans as they arrived to rescue the army of Zobah. This involved David predicting the next move of Zobah's allies after he captured their supply caravan. David's army waits and leads a devastating follow-on ambush against Zobah's allies.

Deception

Effective military leaders master the art of deception. In <u>The Art of War</u>, Sun Tzu explains the commander must trick his enemy in every possible way—making his strengths to appear as weaknesses, and his weaknesses as strengths.

When reading about David in the Bible, it is clear he used deception often . . .

In 1 Samuel 20:5-6, David uses deception when tasking Jonathan with his intelligence gathering mission. He tells Jonathan to report to King Saul he went to his hometown to participate in a family festival. By using deception, David ensures Saul will not be able to find where he is hiding. This protects David. If things go badly for Jonathan, in the worst case scenario, King Saul will be misled into thinking David is in Bethlehem. Thus, David uses deception to throw King Saul further from his trail.

In 1 Samuel 21:2-8, David deceives the priest Ahimelech. He tells the priest he is on a secret mission from King Saul, when he is actually fleeing from him. If Ahimelech knew David was fleeing from King Saul, Ahimelech likely would not have provided food or a sword to David.

Fleeing further, David is captured by the Philistine army and brought before King Achish of Gath (1 Sam. 21:13. David likely fears he will suffer a fate similar to the Judge Samson—who was also captured by the Philistines (Judg. 16:21). Therefore, David decides to act like a madman in the presence of the Philistine king—drooling on himself and scribbling on the wall. The deception is successful: King Achish expels David from his court.

Later, in 1 Samuel 27:8-12, David again uses deception against King Achish for one year and four months. While living in Philistine territory outside the reach of King Saul, David continues to fight for Israel. David leads his army in raids against Israel's enemies near and within Philistine territory. However, when David gives battle reports to King Achish, he falsely reports raids against Israel and her allies. David leaves no one alive to report contrary to his words. Thus, David lives under the jurisdiction of the Philistine king while still fighting for Israel.

When considering the use of deception, it may seem as if this goes against the virtues of honesty and integrity. However, in war you must survive. And the enemy you face will be neither honest nor faithful to you. As a warrior you must learn to conceal your strengths and make your weaknesses appear strong. Only then will you prevail. Deception is a critical battle skill.

Return from war alive. Then take moral inventory of your choices—perhaps with the assistance of a counselor. Do not make the mistake of sharing anything with civilians—except in the case they have strikingly similar personal experiences and have a reputation for gravity, empathy and anonymity. Apart from these rare individuals, it is impossible for civilians to understand your deployment hardships. Don't bother sharing with civilians who have no hope of offering you true empathy and anonymity. Trust a counselor instead.

Decisions & Advisers

In 2 Samuel 16:21, it states David previously relied on the counsel of Ahithophel—which was so highly regarded it was followed as if his counsel were preceding directly from God.

In 2 Samuel 18:3-4, David was dissuaded from leading his army by his three generals—Joab, Abishai and Ittai. If they did not dissuade him, it is likely David would have led his army to confront Absalom's rebellion.

In 2 Samuel 21:15-17, David listens to his subordinate commanders when they urge him to remain away from all future battlefields following David's narrow escape from death—where Abishai killed a Philistine giant to rescue the king.

As seen in the above experiences of David, it helps to have advisers and people to give you counsel based on their experience. Although you will ultimately make the best decision for yourself, you should take care to be fully informed of different perspectives first. This is how you make well-informed decisions. Others may be capable of seeing within ourselves something we cannot. Therefore, listen to your advisers.

Deterring Enemy Attacks

Being good at concealing your position and strength also serves to deter enemies from attacking you.

In 2 Samuel 17:8-9 it was suspected David would be hiding somewhere separate from his troops due to him being wary of traps. In this way, David's reputation of being sneaky deterred his enemies from attempting to find him. They assumed David would be leading them into a trap. Thus, building a reputation of shadiness or sneakiness may actually save your life by dissuading enemies from attacking you.

After all, who would be so unwise to attempt sneaking up on David?

David snuck up on Saul twice—eluding his entire army. So, David's enemies reasoned attempting to sneak up on the stealthy David would surely backfire.

Develop a reputation for being slippery, elusive and cunning. By doing so you will dissuade enemies from daring to attack you. If ever you are attacked, you must make your attackers pay ten-fold. Make the earth melt around them. Word will spread. Then you will be left untouched by other would-be attackers.

Be hard. At all times project confidence and power. All would-be attackers should inherently fear you. As a military leader, when you have interactions with foreign militaries, or if you are viewed from a distance, ensure you are viewed as an absolutely unassailable bulwark—in charge of a unit even more disciplined and powerful. Would-be attackers should fear you. And those who might betray you should cower at the thought of your unit bearing down all its military power upon them.

If ever you are attacked, make the earth melt under your enemy.

Gauge your surroundings. Develop the persona which you believe will be most effective at warding off potential enemy attack.

In my past travels, I have found adopting "craziness" is a good way to ward would-be attackers.

For example, if you are located in a certain position where your presence is known and observed from far off—yell loudly and often. Appear crazed, violent, intimidating—as if you are on a hairpin trigger and about ready to explode at any moment at anything. Put razor wire on everything. Fortify your position like a madman. And perhaps in this way this guise may help you as it helped me. Foreign soldiers who do not understand you will just see you as an insane person who is extreme and violent, and over the top. And by viewing you in this way, they may elect instead to find a softer target.

If you appear powerful, strong and forceful with dominating, boisterous bearing it is most likely an enemy who views you from afar will avoid locking horns with you.

A very good way to deter enemy attacks is to have a "show of force." If you have a ton of extra ammo and if you are at risk of attack because enemy's know where you are, consider doing a range "show of force."

What is the best way to do a show of force?

Call in close air support to fire various munitions at a secluded area next to your location. Potential enemies who view the light display and powerful booms from a distance will be deterred from attacking you—recognizing if they do so they will be destroyed for it.

Discipline & Confrontation

Leadership involves making corrections. Discipline is vital within a military unit. A military unit without discipline falls into chaos. Remember: Whenever there are two or more people, someone is in charge. Concerning discipline, confrontation and punishment, I have several things for you to consider . . .

As a leader, your standard mode of communication should be *frank and direct*.

In 1 Samuel 24:7, David rebukes his soldiers when they speak of killing King Saul (see also 1 Sam. 26:9).

Then, in 1 Samuel 30:22-25, David rebukes the troublemakers in his army who attempted to deprive the 200 exhausted soldiers of their share in battle plunder. David declares all his soldiers will have an equal share. At this point it is remarkable David would rebuke his men—considering they just spoke of stoning him a day earlier. However, David's effectiveness as a battle commander demonstrated he was worthy of respect. Therefore, the troublemakers quickly conceded to David's rebuke.

However, some difficult situations require *finesse* . . .

In 1 Samuel 30:6-9, David responds to his soldiers' mutiny by directly addressing the grievance rather than the soldiers themselves. Discernment was required to successfully navigate this situation. If David attempted to punish the individual soldiers who mentioned stoning him, it is likely his army would have been divided or disbanded. However, by addressing the grievance and leading his men to resolve the situation he indirectly dissuaded the mutiny. At times, the best decision is to quickly resolve the grievance itself, rather than engaging with the individuals.

At times when it is not prudent to judge a subordinate, take comfort in the fact God will bring about justice Himself. When someone does bad things, bad things have a tendency to come back to them . . . karma and all that.

In 2 Samuel 3:28-29, David asks God to judge Joab for his murder of Abner. In this case, David elects to look to God for help rather than ordering the execution of Judah's army general.

However, David does make Joab participate in the funeral procession of Abner (2 Sam. 3:31). Perhaps this was embarrassing for Joab—leading him many years later to directly challenge David following the death of David's son, Absalom (2 Sam.

19:7). So, even in the case you cannot directly punish an offender, find alternate ways to compel him to see his wrongdoing. If done properly, the offender may come to a realization of his wrongdoing.

Give justice to people when it is in your power to do it . . .

In 2 Samuel 14:4, David provides grievance resolution for a citizen. Although this was a feigned grievance, the fact David held court for citizens demonstrates he was concerned with providing justice to his people.

Separate yourself from the wickedness of others—publicly placing the blame upon those responsible . . .

In 2 Samuel 3:22-27, Joab plots against and kills Abner. David counters Joab's action by publicly declaring Joab's guilt through a funeral (2 Sam. 3:28-39).

Punishment for severe crimes should be severe. The goal is to enforce discipline throughout the entire unit. By punishing offenders it sends a clear message to the unit that this type of behavior will not be tolerated.

In 2 Samuel 1:16, David orders the execution of a man after he declares he killed King Saul.

Then, in 2 Samuel 4:5-12, David orders the execution of the two men who murdered the king of Israel.

In cases where it is appropriate to punish a suspected offender, always read the person his rights. Send him to speak with a military lawyer to ensure he is fully aware of his rights. Then do the paperwork and figure out the right punishment for the offense to make your recommendation to the commanding officer. To determine the appropriate punishment, simply look in your unit's records to determine what previous service-members who committed a similar crime were awarded as punishment.

If at any point in time you are accused of a crime—no matter how big or small—do not speak. Respectfully ask to speak to a military lawyer. Many people choose to speak and immediately put themselves in positions where they admit to wrongdoing. Before you choose to speak, consult with a military lawyer first.

If you have done wrong, it is your choice how to approach the situation. As you determine, you can choose to accept fault and take your punishment, or ask for court martial trial. This is your right. But do not sell yourself short of your options by speaking too quickly. Carefully weigh out your options first.

<u>Distrust & Trust</u>

In unconventional warfare you can expect to get screwed over by non-uniformed people. At some point or another you will likely have someone betray you.

In unconventional warfare, the real bad guys are the ones you will never meet. They remain hidden. They simply blackmail others into doing attacks for them. So, no matter how secure a location may appear, realize this dynamic is present. To stay safe, your default should be to distrust people until they have earned your trust.

Throughout the Psalms we see David constantly suspected others of plotting against him. Although this is not normal for an average citizen; distrusting people is a healthy trait for any successful military commander—especially in the ancient world.

A military commander who expects betrayal can plan ahead to protect himself and his troops. Overall, David's distrust of people protected him from all the plots of Saul, in addition to protecting him during Absalom's rebellion. Although David would misunderstand people at many times, his social impairment allowed him to see through the potentially negative motives of people. Therefore, we can be certain David's distrust of people saved his life—many, many times.

Consider motives . . .
A military commander should always consider the potential motives of people. Ask yourself . . .

"What would this person have to gain for betraying us?"

"Why would this person want to betray me?"

"Could someone be using this person as a pawn or informant?"

Asking such questions allows a military commander to plan accordingly to prevent overly trusting a person who could be compromised. In other words, we have heard it said, *"I would not trust him further than I can throw him."*

So, start there. Trust a person only when they are in arm's reach of you—while you can observe everything they are doing. But the moment you let that person out of your sight, be wary of him. You should be thinking to yourself: *Where did this person just go? Did he just grab a weapon? What's in his pocket? . . .* And so on.

Is this type of thinking exhausting? Absolutely it is!

But, in the places where the military may send you, there are many people who have years of resentment built up within themselves. And to those people, your life means absolutely nothing. Do not be deceived about that. You have no reason to trust anyone—even if your boss says you should trust him.

Your intuition will guide you. Trust your gut—and immediately act on it. If you feel something is fishy, give orders to deescalate the situation immediately. Don't allow your life to be gambled away as a pawn to someone's resentment. Protect yourself and your people. Determine the trustworthiness of an individual and allow that to guide all your interactions with him. In this way you will keep safe.

In 1 Samuel 20:8, David shows he had a distrust for people—even those closest to him. It is possible David thought even Jonathan betrayed him—as it seems to indicate in Psalm 55:13.

Also, in 1 Samuel 21:2, David distrusts the priest, Ahimelech—choosing to tell him that he is on a secret mission, when in fact he was fleeing from King Saul.

However, David fails to distrust Doeg in 1 Samuel 21:7, resulting in his betrayal to Saul. Later, in 1 Samuel 22:22, David regrets allowing this oversight—blaming himself for the deaths of all the citizens of Nob.

Most notable was the betrayal of Abiathar the priest. Abiathar's betrayal is perhaps the most significant and unexpected for David—playing with the memories of David, making him wonder why he so quickly trusted Abiathar in his youth. David and Abiathar were originally bonded in grief for the loss of the citizens of Nob. Throughout his travels, Abiathar remains close to David—offering him key advice at different times. Unfortunately, at the end of David's reign, Abiathar betrays David after many years of faithful service (1 Kings 1:7). This betrayal is severe—cutting all the way to David's youth. The priest, Abiathar, with whom David often shared religious fellowship and prayer during his travels finally lifts up his heel against the aging king (Psa. 41:9).

Distrust sketchy people who "could" be lying . . .

In 2 Samuel 1:16, David orders the execution of a man who reports he killed King Saul. The fact the man fled from battle, further into Philistine territory, to David's camp in Ziklag, likely tipped David off to the man's duplicity. If the man were faithful to Israel, he would have fled from the battle in the opposite direction—toward Israel. David distrusts the man's motive for killing Saul, faulting him for failing to attempt to save Saul.

47

In 2 Samuel 4:5-12, David distrusts the men who murdered the king of Israel. The two men say kind words to David, as if they were friends of his kingship. David saw through their veiled wickedness—determining their action was unrighteous. He orders their execution, thus preventing the infiltration of his court with these wicked men.

Don't trust the words of people: Sift through their words, carefully comparing them with their actions. Only then can you see through the duplicity of others.

Decide for yourself . . .

In 1 Samuel 25:5-12, David sends messengers to speak with a rich man, named Nabal. Although it is appropriate to send messengers at times, a leader should be wary of using messengers in situations where a likely/potential conflict could occur. In this case it was not wise for David to use messengers. David had no contract with Nabal, and he was under no compulsion to provide food for David's army. Thus, it was not reasonable for David to send messengers to receive payment when there was no contract in place. David should have went in person to Nabal.

Therefore, it is much more likely David used this entire situation to psychologically manipulate the payment for his soldiers' services. When considering David's use of deception before King Achish and also before Ahimelech the priest, it is likely David used deception against Nabal (1 Sam. 21:2, 12-14).

Why not? Suspecting he would not be paid, David could have sent messengers as a part of his plot. Once receiving the report from his messengers, David feigned threats to compel a favorable response from Nabal's clan.

Of course, we cannot know for sure, but I think this is a good option when considering David's tactics and the situation presented. Guessing he would not receive a favorable response upon his request for food from Nabal, he sends messengers, then responds in a way to compel the desired reaction from Nabal's clan. David distrusts Nabal, so he schemes to feign anger by threatening to kill all the men in Nabal's household. The feigned anger accomplishes the original goal—obtaining food for his troops. So, was David mistreated by Nabal, or was this scenario the result of David carefully using distrust and deception to psychologically manipulate Nabal's clan into providing food for his army?

What do you think?

. . . And if you cannot see it, this means the deception was utterly seamless.

As a military leader you may have to interact with very duplicitous people. Be cunning in your interactions. Be seamless. Protect your people. If anyone is being deceptive it should be you. You should be the one pulling hidden strings to manipulate those around you. Do not allow yourself to be the puppet who is dangled. Be in control of your surroundings so you can survive. Doubt everyone. Survive.

<u>Encryption, Coded Communication & Whispering</u>

In the military radios are encrypted to prevent enemies from intercepting transmissions. During my years in war we would refer to encrypted radio transmissions as being "in the green." But non-encrypted radio transmissions were referred to as "red." In other words, on green frequencies you could pass the numbers of grid coordinates and other sensitive information. However, when speaking on red frequencies, grid coordinate numbers would each need to be encrypted by using the letters of a daily code word—known only by friendlies with a secret clearance.

In 1 Samuel 20:20-22, Jonathan and David develop a code to communicate a message. They made it appear as if Jonathan were speaking to another soldier aloud, when in fact he was speaking to David.

Always be wary of how information may be used against you. When you are in doubt, make sure you code your communication.

It is easy to develop coded communication—even if you do not use radios. Perhaps the simplest way to code your communication is by whispering. Speak quietly when you know your words could get you and your people in trouble. The best leaders know when to raise their voices and also when to whisper. And at times you are required to say something which straddles the gray line, speak it so softly that the other will need to lean toward you— barely hearing what you say. In that case, make sure you speak it to only one other—leaving no situation where there are multiple witnesses to the words you speak. This allows you to deny and step back from the words if they are discovered—leaving only a single witness, and never more than that. Thus you will preserve your anonymity if required to go beyond boundary.

A quick word about "popping smoke" . . .

If you are ever using colored smoke to mark a helicopter landing zone, never say the color of the smoke over the radio. Tell the pilot the LZ is marked with smoke. Then wait for him to report the specific color of smoke in sight. When he says it is in sight, tell the pilot, "Continue."

It would be terrible for you to tell the pilot the color of smoke. For example, if the smoke used is red, and you say that over the radio, then your enemy who intercepts your radio transmission could also pop red smoke. In this case, the helicopter pilot may be unwittingly guided to the wrong location. This is why you should never say the color of smoke.

. . . This is a small example, but it fully illustrates the importance of coding all communications. You never know who is listening.

Always think how information could be used against you. Then protect it at all costs from compromise.

Extra Duties

In 1 Samuel 16:11, the young David stayed in the field working while his entire family visited with the prophet Samuel. Whether ordered to do so or not, this shows David was willing to work extra to allow others to enjoy themselves. He took upon himself extra duties beyond his fair share.

In 1 Samuel 17:15 it states David had two jobs. He served as both the armor bearer for the king, and also as the family shepherd.

On a positive side, there is a large benefit to be gained in extra duties. Although one may work many hours, having extra responsibilities can provide clarity and focus for the other one. Having additional duties prevents tunnel vision common to people who have all their eggs in one basket.

For example, as David approached the battle line, he found the entire army of Israel was likeminded in their terror of Goliath (1 Sam. 17:24). However, David being separate from the army prevented him from developing the same tunnel vision afflicting the echo chamber of Saul's army. David's time away from the battlefield allowed him to approach the situation with fresh perspective. While the entire army stood mystified, David immediately visualized a solution to the Goliath problem.

So, never look at extra duties as being irrelevant. Being able to step away from your regular duties may give you a sharper perspective upon your return. Moreover, your willingness to work beyond your fair share allows you to gain honor among your fellows and superiors. And, having a good work ethic is an outstanding way to honor the warriors who have served before you and your own family clan. Never shy away from extra work, but accept it enthusiastically.

Faith & Proof of God

In 1 Samuel 17:46, David states the world will know there is a God in Israel when he defeats Goliath. Often when skeptics ask for "proof of God's existence" in present day, they are looking for objective facts. However, for the people of the Bible, faith in God is subjective and personal. Thus, David points out people should know God exists because those who trust Him are victorious in battle.

For the ancient warrior who leaves the battlefield intact, his "survival" is the only proof required for God's existence. In the midst of a violent world, "survival" was the grandest of all proofs. However, in present day where survival is completely taken for granted, people are confused on the purpose of "faith"—thinking God must be proven to the faithless. But, faith is about survival; not objective "proof."

It appears humans forgot this original form of Bible faith—which is centered upon survival. In my work, I introduce readers to the ancient faith of David—a faith which allows one to survive battlefields.

At its core, faith is subjective and personal. Faith is something that does not need to be "proven" to others. Faith is not something that fits in a glass jar, or that can be weighed on a scale.

Rather, faith is the incredible means through which ancient people survived trauma. The purpose of faith is found in its ability to help people survive situations where they would not have survived.

Concerning David, faith in God was the only way he was able to survive. If he did not have "faith" he would have perished. Faith helped him persevere—constantly drawing from the bottomless supernatural well provided by God.

However, in the modern world of comforts, human society has grown so accustomed to ease people have altogether forgotten what it means to suffer. Our ancient ancestors were accustomed to suffering, trauma and tragedy, so faith was naturally born as the only means to survive otherwise impossible physical situations through depersonalization and derealization.

But, when one is unaccustomed to suffering, faith become divorced from its original connection with trauma. This explains why it seems no one understands faith anymore. Look no further than the myriad conversations and debates today where Christians are asked to "prove God exists."

The power of faith is that it is subjective and personal. The person "believes." That personal belief requires no objective validation or approval from consensus. My personal trauma has brought me to "believe." It is irrelevant whether another person agrees with me.

So, when understanding faith and its total dependence upon trauma, "proving God exists" is a venture altogether foreign to Bible faith. The Bible invites you to "believe," but it is altogether unconcerned with objectively proving anything to the skeptical. Believe it or do not.

The pathway to understanding faith is to suffer without hope of physical respite. When stuck in suffering to the point of exhaustion, then the person can be ushered into the hope of faith. In the midst of trauma, faith emerges. It is something personal; not something to be proven to those surrounded by the comforts of this world.

This is the means to establishing a deep, personal connection with God. When your faith helps you survive, your faith becomes most precious. And, in its great utility, it matters not what others think of your faith. They may scratch their heads; while your body surges with waves of supernatural power.

If you want this spiritual power in Christ, it is offered to you freely . . .

"Let the one who is thirsty come; and let the one who wishes take the free gift of the water of life." (Revelation 22:17b)

Family

Family dynamics can present difficulties for the warrior. It is good to make sure one's family is taken care of prior to leaving on a deployment. As one ventures to lead troops, they must venture to properly lead their own families.

Although he made mistakes, David shows us how we should be mindful of our relationships with our parents, spouses and children. . . .

Responsibility for Parents

As a child, David had problems with his parents (Psa. 22:10; 27:10; 69:8). However, he did not neglect his duties. Throughout David's childhood, he served as the family shepherd. He even continued his duties as shepherd while concurrently serving as armor bearer for King Saul.

Later, in 1 Samuel 22:1-4, David's parents come to visit him while he is staying within the Moabite stronghold. David's parents were elderly at this point. At this time David asks the Moabite king for permission to allow his parents to remain within the city while he is absent. Perhaps this is the last visit David enjoys with his parents before they pass away.

Responsibility for Spouses and Children

In 1 Samuel 27:2-6, David and his army of 600 men find a permanent home base in Ziklag. They bring their families to this Philistine city, where they remain for one year and four months. Following the destruction of Ziklag, David's army and all their families travel with him to Hebron—where he is anointed as king of Judah (2 Sam. 2:3-4).

In 2 Samuel 5:13-16, it says David took more wives and concubines. In the ancient world, clan leaders would take multiple wives so they could have more sons to build their number of fighters rapidly. David adopts this practice—leading to the birth of many sons and daughters.

In 2 Samuel 11:27, although David messed up in his treatment of Bathsheba and Uriah, he did not neglect her in her pregnancy. He married her after Uriah was dead.

Last, in 2 Samuel 7:12-16, God declares through Nathan the prophet that David's descendants will serve as kings after him. At the end of David's reign, he allows Solomon to serve concurrently with him as king—enabling Solomon to benefit fully from David's mentorship. Ultimately, this succession of kings will result in the arrival of the Messiah king, the Lord Jesus.

Family Crisis

In 2 Samuel 12:24, David comforts his wife, Bathsheba, after the death of their first son. He made sure she was not grieving alone.

In 2 Samuel 13:1-20, David's son raped his half-sister. As a result his family had problems lasting for many years. David was angry, yet he failed to take action to punish his son.

Later in 2 Samuel 13:28, David's son, Absalom, murdered David's son, Amnon. This was done to avenge the rape of Absalom's sister, Tamar, by Amnon.

During a national rebellion, David took measures to protect his family. In 2 Samuel 15:16, David brings his household with him when fleeing from Absalom's rebellion.

In 2 Samuel 20:3 it says David took measures to provide for his concubines who were abused during Absalom's rebellion. He provided them a guarded house following his restoration to the kingship.

Throughout your life, your family will doubtlessly undergo changes. And, as relationships often teach us, no one is perfect. We all make mistakes. Nonetheless, a warrior should be concerned with his family—making them a priority. So, be there for your family during different stages in life. Do your best.

<u>Fear</u>

In 1 Samuel 21:12, David is afraid when captured and brought before Achish, the Philistine king of Gath. In this case, his healthy fear inspired him to take action. David feigned madness in the king's presence—inspiring the king to let him go. So, for the warrior, healthy fear can be a life saver.

In 1 Samuel 23:3-4 we see fear can be managed with confidence and courage. Although David's soldiers were fearful, David's confidence in the Lord gave his army courage to attack the Philistines at Keilah. Thus, fear can be mastered by confidence and courage.

In 1 Samuel 30:6, David was distressed in spirit when his army discussed mutiny against him. This fear prompted David to action—where he prayed and made effective decisions, leading to the resolution of the soldiers' grievance. Their families were rescued from the Amalekite raiders and the soldiers remained faithful to David.

In 2 Samuel 6:9, David was fearful of the Lord after the death of Uzzah, the priest. Uzzah died for an irreverent act—where he grabbed the ark with his hand. David likely feared further judgment of God upon himself for failing to properly oversee the priests' procedures for moving the ark. Perhaps the fear of David is what turned the wrath of God away from him. In the wake of Uzzah's irreverent act,

David made sure to be especially reverent—to the point of having a healthy fear of God. David waits for God's anger to subside before he resumes the ark transport (2 Sam. 6:12).

During times where you feel fearful you should be especially careful. Think, pray and decide what to do. Then muster the courage to execute your plan.

Ferocity

As previously discussed, a significant difference between David and Saul is found in the structure of their armies. Whereas Saul preferred to do things on his own; David took time to develop subordinate leaders, called "mighty men," who could serve in his stead (2 Sam. 23:8-38). Whereas Saul had no champion who could fight Goliath for his honor; David gathered an entire court of champions around him—each capable of felling giants (2 Sam. 21:15-20).

In 2 Samuel 17:8 it states David and his men were as fierce as wild bears robbed of their cubs. This is a remarkable reputation—capable of dissuading enemies from attempting an attack on David's army. Rather than remaining valorous alone, David took action to develop ferocity within all his troops. As a result, over time, David's entire army inherited this incredible trait from their king.

In your military leadership, do likewise. Be ferocious and train your warriors to be ferocious.

In the wilderness, a bear is perhaps the most terrifying creature. Once it begins its charge toward a man, nothing can slow its advance. Even gunshots are ineffective. Unlike large cat predators with killer instincts to grab the throat of their prey; a bear altogether lacks grace. The prey of a bear dies in agony from a brutal mauling. In other words, to say

David and his army were like bears was to recognize their utterly inescapable, unrelenting, agonizingly powerful battlefield prowess. Once provoked, David's army had a reputation of absolutely mauling their enemies upon the battlefield—battering them into submission.

Do you desire this power?

Then be ferocious. Train your warriors to be ferocious. Put them in charge of others to pass on this trait.

<u>Flanking Attack</u>

In 2 Samuel 5:23, David is directed to use a circling maneuver to position his army to attack the Philistines. David's ability to quickly move his army allowed him to wrest initiative from his enemies, keeping them off-balanced and forcing them to their culminating point.

In some cases military tactics can be confusing. But allow me to simplify how to pull off a successful attack—especially if you are new to military leadership. . . .

Divide your attacking force into three groups. I don't care how small your group is. . . . If you have six soldiers, put them in three groups of two. Or if you have 20, divide them into two groups of seven and one group of six.

Got it?

Then, one group should fire and move near the front of the enemy. The goal is for this first group to keep the enemy pinned down by gunfire. This first group is tasked with direct assault.

Then your second group circles up one of the sides of the enemy—attacking them from their flank. If the first group does a good job pinning down the enemy, and if the second group moves quickly, the flank will be successful.

Keep your third group as a reserve—waiting until just the right moment to send them to a specific point or specific action. Basically your third group should be ready to pounce on the biggest area of vulnerability. For example, if you expect your enemy will flee, then you could have your third group set an ambush on the enemy's likely avenue of retreat.

When considering military tactics, this approach is the most simple and effective. The first group is direct assault; the second group flanks; and the third group is placed wherever you need them most on the battlefield.

This is a very basic tactic scheme you can use anywhere—no matter how small your unit. Even if you only have three people—you need to designate one person as direct fire, one as flank and the third as reserve to exploit the enemy.

Remember this. Don't ever make the mistake of just telling your people to attack in mass. Divide them by three and use this format always.

Follow-on Attacks

After a successful raid you may feel inclined to sit on the enemy's equipment as you eat their chow. But don't do this. Keep moving to protect yourself.

The enemy may have reinforcements on the way. Think about the direction from which they will be arriving. Then set traps and an ambush to intercept the enemy reinforcements unaware.

If you have opportunity, capture one of the enemy's radiomen and radio further misleading information to the reinforcements who are on the way. Walk your enemy further into your trap— thereby fully exploiting the enemy with a devastating follow-on attack.

In 2 Samuel 8:4, David's army ambushes the forces of Hadadezer, king of Zobah, as they moved to solidify their control along the Euphrates River. It appears this army included a supply caravan—due to the large numbers of horses and chariots.

Then, David's army set an ambush for the next group of Arameans (2 Sam. 8:5). David's army ambushed the Arameans as they arrived to rescue the army of Zobah. This involved David predicting the next move of Zobah's allies after he captured their supply caravan. David's army waits and leads a devastating follow-on ambush against Zobah's allies.

Food

Of course warriors cannot be discussed without discussing food.

In your military travels make sure you know where your provisions are coming from. Take measures to stockpile food and water in the case supplies are cut off.

There are several instances which describe how the warrior David provisioned food and provided for his people . . .

In 1 Samuel 21:3-6, David gathers provisions from the Lord's house. With no other food available, David asks the priest for the sacred bread from the altar.

In 1 Samuel 25:4-5, David's army protects local shepherds while they are camping in the wilderness. At the completion of the season, David asks the owner to provide food for his army.

In 1 Samuel 30:11-12, David uses figs and raisins to revive the hungry Egyptian in the wilderness. This provides us insight into the food used by warriors when they became exhausted—figs, raisins and water.

In 2 Samuel 3:20, David has a feast prepared for Abner, the general of Israel, who arrives in Hebron with twenty men.

In 2 Samuel 6:19, David provides provisions for those worshipping the Lord during the transportation of the ark. He provides bread, dates and raisins for all the people.

<u>Funerals & Grieving</u>

In David's life we see the importance of funerals. After the Nob incident—where all the citizens were slaughtered, David felt responsible (1 Sam. 22:22). He was unable to attend funerals because he was fleeing from Saul.

Later however, David copes much better after he is able to fully grieve with losses—such as the deaths of Saul, Jonathan and Abner (2 Sam. 1:17-27; 3:28-39).

Funerals give survivors the opportunity to re-frame events in their proper context by listening to the stories of other survivors. If David were able to attend funerals at Nob, it would have dispelled his false view of personal culpability.

Therefore, in all cases, if your conscience is drawing you to grieve, see this as a vital opportunity to mentally organize events to come to grips with them. Don't neglect your conscience. Don't allow false perceptions to build over the years. Stay in touch with your conscience. Attend funerals.

Garrisons

The point of garrisons and tribute is to render an enemy territory incapable of again amassing sufficient military force. On a large scale, whenever your military achieves a victory, make plans immediately to ensure you will not be put in a similar situation again. In this way, garrisons provide a constant check on the amassing of military power by an enemy (2 Sam. 10:15). As soon as a contingency is detected, the garrison force can immediately address the problem. This ensures all battles will remain in foreign territories rather than your own territories.

Throughout David's reign he consistently used garrisons in order to effectively hold territory. In 2 Samuel 8:1, David seizes a chief city from the Philistines—likely creating a garrison within it.

In 2 Samuel 8:6, David puts garrisons in Aramean territories after defeating them in battle.

In 2 Samuel 8:13-14, David sets up garrisons in previously held enemy territory after his military victory in the Valley of Salt.

Last, in 2 Samuel 12:31, David placed garrisons within Ammonite territory after capturing the city, Rabbah. In these garrisons, David's army supervised labor within Ammonite settlements.

If ever you fight in a region long term, you must have a long term plan to keep enemy activity suppressed. Garrisons accomplish that purpose. Once you gain victory in a region do not allow your enemy to once again gain a foothold.

<u>Gear</u>

Always pack light. Take only what you need.

In 1 Samuel 17:38-39, David refuses to use the bulky armor of King Saul. Instead, he opts for simple gear and weapons.

In 1 Samuel 17:40, David uses only his shepherd staff and slingshot in the champion battle with Goliath. After felling Goliath with his slingshot, David uses the giant's sword to behead him.

In 1 Samuel 18:4 Jonathan gives David military gear, including a robe, belt, sword and bow.

As much as possible, keep your gear simple. You will see others who like to keep getting the newest gear. Remember anything you add to your gear, you will have to carry. And if the advantage it provides is not worth having to lug it around for months, then do not buy it. You may be required by your unit to take certain gear with you on deployment, but if you are not "required" to take unnecessary items—don't. Bring extra ammo instead.

God Fights for David

Depersonalization

In 2 Samuel 7:22, we see David believed his God to be completely unique and more powerful than any other "gods." This exclusivity in his religious beliefs would have granted David additional courage and confidence on the battlefield. Whereas other men may have thought it possible for the gods of others to defeat their own god; David altogether rejected this thought. In David's mind, there is no other supernatural being who is a match for his own God. Thus, David wielded an incredible spiritual enhancement to his battlefield abilities. He believed himself invincible through his direct association with God.

In 1 Samuel 17:37, David viewed God as fighting from within him. In 1 Samuel 20:15-16, Jonathan views the Lord as fighting through the actions of David.

Essentially, David viewed his physical actions as God's actions. So, God worked in and through David to deliver David. This is called "depersonalization"—where a person experiences feeling detached from himself as if he is in a dream or an outside observer. Thus, when David fought he viewed his actions as a combination of his actions and the actions of God within him.

When swinging a weapon, David would have perceived *both* the sensation of performing the action, while also feeling detached from it. Within the PTSD mind of David, he interpreted those feelings of detachment as instances where God was momentarily taking over from *within* him. David was completely convinced God was fighting *through* him.

In other words, David was not being poetic or merely giving God glory in a religious sense. Rather, when David glorifies God for his military victories, David is explaining how he felt. David's PTSD depersonalization caused him to feel detached from his own actions—and within that detachment he sensed God actually moving his body for him.

I hope that is clear. When a person understands this about how the minds of ancient warriors worked and how they were impacted by depersonalization, suddenly the Bible makes sense. Depersonalization explains Bible prophecy perfectly—particularly in its ability for prophets to "feel" for themselves events experienced in the body of the Lord Jesus.

Ancient people experienced trauma and survived through PTSD. The symptom "PTSD depersonalization" transformed how they felt within themselves and viewed the world around them.

Simple, but those who are not familiar with suffering cannot understand. And, as a result of their lack of psychological understanding, they wrongly think David was being merely poetic in his attribution of his victories to God. However, David was not being poetic; he was explaining how he *actually felt* as God was moving his body. But, I digress . . .

So, what benefit is depersonalization to a warrior?

Depersonalization allows the spiritual warrior to override physical exhaustion. The spiritual warrior becomes capable of toggling in and out of attachment to the physical. When exhausted the spiritual warrior can trust God to take over.

On a battlefield, this allows the spiritual warrior to push himself much further than his actual physical limitations. Thus, on a battlefield depersonalization can save the warrior's life. In other words, a warrior with depersonalization can overcome physical limitations through his mind.

In my book, <u>Dear David: Learning to See God through PTSD, Anxiety and Depression</u>, I trace "depersonalization" throughout the life of David as a major source of his spirituality and combat abilities. Moreover, I demonstrate how depersonalization became a major component of Bible prophecy, following David's example. Not only did depersonalization enhance David's fighting abilities,

Biblical faith as it exists today is a direct result of David's depersonalization.

Those who practice Biblical faith unwittingly adopt PTSD symptoms—particularly derealization and depersonalization, as taught by the prophets and apostles. Thus, Bible faith itself is based on trauma survival. This is a good thing and anyone who desires to understand the underpinnings of religion would be wise to look into this topic more deeply. When understanding this it becomes clear the Bible was written to help us survive the trauma of this fallen world through Christ.

For complete study on the topic of PTSD, consult the DSM-5 (Diagnostic and Statistical Manual of Mental Disorders, 5th Ed., American Psychiatric Association, American Psychiatric Publishing, 2013).

God Defends David

In 1 Samuel 25:38-39, the Lord strikes Nabal so he dies. David interprets Nabal's death as the result of Nabal's insult against him. So, David views actions around him as the result of God's action on his behalf. Since Nabal insulted David, David views Nabal's natural death as the result of God defending his honor.

This may seem bizarre, however there is power contained within this type of thinking. To view all events as being directed by God allows a warrior to be in tune with everything in his environment. In other words, if I am joined to God in faith, and if God is moving everything around me, then I am in tune with my entire environment.

Thus, the spiritual warrior develops a perception of the world around him as being in a sense an extension of himself. Actions which occur do not surprise God, but are directed and incorporated into His plan. And since the warrior is himself a part of that plan, he can be at peace in the midst of chaos occurring around him.

Try it for yourself. When events happen, view them as somehow being a part of God's plan—as He works all things according to good purpose (Rom. 8:28). The spiritual warrior harnesses this thought and uses it to his advantage.

God Protects & Presides over David

In 1 Samuel 19:19-24, the Holy Spirit helps David escape from Saul. As King Saul's men pursued David, the Holy Spirit entered into them, supernaturally preventing them from continuing on the road. Thus, God fought for David by intercepting Saul's forces—thereby giving David more time to escape.

In 1 Samuel 23:4, God tells David He will give him military victory over the Philistines at Keilah. It is worded as if the Lord Himself will preside over the battle—choosing to hand over David's enemies to him.

In 1 Samuel 23:7, Saul presumes God will "hand over" David to him because David is within the city of Keilah. However, God provides a warning to David through Abiathar—delivering him from Saul's hand (1 Sam. 23:9-12). This shows God protects David in a special way.

In 1 Samuel 23:14 we see God is viewed as presiding over all military battles. Thus, God is in the position to "hand over" one army to another in defeat. God delivers David by refusing to hand him over to Saul.

In 1 Samuel 23:26-28, David narrowly escapes Saul at the Desert of Maon. In the context, it is assumed the Lord orchestrates circumstances to deliver David by getting Saul to abandon his pursuit.

In 1 Samuel 26:8, 23, David and Abishai interpret their successful sneaking mission as God handing over Saul to David. This demonstrates David thought of God presiding over his military actions.

In 1 Samuel 29:8, David is prevented from entering the battle between Israel and the Philistines. In this way, God withdraws his favor from Israel—dooming King Saul on the battlefield. If David entered this battle, God's favor would have rested upon David. So to allow for the downfall of

Saul, God orchestrates circumstances to ensure David was not permitted to enter the battle.

In 1 Samuel 30:8, God tells David He will give him victory against the Amalekite raiders who destroyed Ziklag.

In 1 Samuel 30:23, David states God protected and granted his army victory against the Amalekites.

In 2 Samuel 5:19-20, David prays and God directs him to attack the Philistine army at Baal Perazim. Following this battle, God gives David specific instructions on how to successfully attack the Philistines in the Valley of Rephaim (2 Sam. 5:22-24).

In 2 Samuel 7:1, David credits God for giving him temporary peace. Thus, this is indirectly ascribing credit to God for the military victories of David.

In 2 Samuel 7:9, God states He cut off all David's enemies.

In 2 Samuel 8:11-12, David dedicates war plunder to the Lord's house—including gold, silver and bronze. With these dedications, David acknowledges his military victories belong to the Lord (2 Sam. 8:14).

In 2 Samuel 17:14, it is declared the Lord halted Absalom's rebellion to save David.

God as Supreme Judge

In 2 Samuel 3:28-29, David asks God to judge Joab for his murder of Abner. In this case, David elects to look to God for help rather than ordering the execution of Judah's army general. In this way, David looks to God as the Supreme Judge to render judgment on his behalf.

Indeed, as a warrior there will be much around you which is truly beyond your control. Thus, the spiritual warrior becomes capable of rising above injustices and problems by resting his mind upon God. Somehow God will make sense of all things— meting out judgment and reward in just measures.

Thus, by fixing his mind upon God's eventual justice, the warrior is able to remove from himself perplexing thoughts about problems around him. He becomes free to focus on the task at hand—doing his own job with diligence and trusting God to deal with everything which is beyond his control.

<u>God's Will</u>

It is one thing to do an action because it is a good option. However, when one believes God Himself is directing his action, this allows the individual to be solid in his actions.

David ever sought spiritual guidance for his upcoming battles. By praying and seeking the counsel of his priest or prophet, David gained incredible courage and confidence in his next steps.

When David moved, he did so with supernatural confidence—with power surging through each step. His battlefield actions were divinely guided, giving him unshakable confidence. Thus, a practiced spiritual warrior is capable of great focus—drawing supernatural power from beyond the physical veil. David's spirituality was so powerful he viewed God as a fortress of protection, guiding him in his actions. David indeed walked by faith, not by sight (2 Cor. 5:7).

In 2 Samuel 5:20, 24, the heavenly army helps David on the battlefield. David's fighting is accompanied with the supernatural waters and spiritual marching of the heavenly army.

Throughout his battles David ever moved in concert with an unseen power—manipulating physical things before him. David was not a mere physical warrior. Rather, he was a spiritual warrior with the capability of bearing forth God's power onto the battlefield. God channeled His power through David onto the battlefield. This is how the warrior should view himself—as a channel for God's power, serving as an instrument to shape the world around him.

What would it have been like to fight David?

David was a physically proficient warrior. He was swift and elusive. But his most notable trait was his spirituality.

In 2 Samuel 7:9, God declares He cut off all David's enemies—which means David viewed all his victories as the direct result of God's power working through him. It is this conviction which would have given David an edge over all his opponents. A person who fights—being convinced they are called by God and empowered by Him—will be most unassailable when matched with basic physical proficiency. Ultimately, religious conviction made David push himself harder than his opponents—which made him victorious in all his battles.

In summary, if one believes God is with him, he has an edge over those who do not hold such beliefs. The person who believes he is divinely empowered will fight harder—being convinced of God's strength surging through his body.

If you want to become a warrior, embrace the power of God. Look for His guidance and follow His instructions. That is the sure path to victory. And within this path there is a guarantee: God promises to always walk with you—helping you every step of the way, no matter how difficult. Allow yourself to be empowered by God.

<u>Grief & Mourning</u>

When you lose someone, grieve. Often out of a sense of bravado or obligation warriors will refrain from mourning. However, it is important you do not sever your connection with your own emotions.

Although it may not be appropriate to grieve in all places, make sure you go to a place where you can grieve. Allow yourself to cry. This will help you stay in contact with your emotions.

In the Bible there are many examples where the warrior, David, cried. And, since he cried, you can also cry . . .

In 2 Samuel 12:16-19, David fasted and grieved for his sick son.

In 2 Samuel 13:31, David tears his clothes, lays down on the ground and grieves when hearing his son, Absalom, murdered his son, Amnon.

In 2 Samuel 15:30-31, David wept, covered his head and walked barefoot as he fled from Absalom's rebellion.

In 2 Samuel 18:33-19:4, David grieved and wept after hearing of the death of his son, Absalom.

As a warning, if you get into the habit of denying your tears, it becomes more difficult to cry. If you deny your emotions over and over again, eventually they stop "speaking" to you.

To keep your heart tender and capable of empathy, never lose sight of your emotions. You can be tough, but you must also find ways where you can maintain your vulnerability—where you can feel your own beating heart. Remember you are not just a battle-hardened warrior. You are human. Allow yourself to be human.

If you have a military job which requires you to set aside your emotion, find an outlet where you can continue to practice your human emotions. Volunteer somewhere in the community. Practice religion. Read the Scriptures. Overall, stay in tune with your emotions.

If your emotions stop speaking to you, it is difficult to beckon their reemergence. So, put in the work to maintain the emotional parts of your heart—no matter how tough you may be.

Grieve with passion when it is time to grieve.

<u>History, Heritage & Tradition</u>

David viewed himself as serving in the succession of the national Judges who went before him (1 Sam. 16:13). As such, David served in the tradition of those who served his nation before him. So, just as the Judges looked to God's Spirit within them to provide strength to complete their assigned tasks, David also looked to God as the source of all his power.

This is an important point. Traditions are a source of courage for warriors. Our nation's history inspires us to press on when things get difficult.

I believe this is the foundational reason why soldiers wear both their last name and the name of their service on their uniform. These labels serve to constantly remind the warrior they are serving as a representative for both their family clan and for the service itself.

Concerning representing one's family, the warrior bears his last name upon his uniform to honor his ancestors who lived and died before him. As such, the warrior should reflect with every action whether his actions bring honor upon those within his bloodline. Even in the case previous generations caused dishonor to fall upon his name, the warrior now bears the responsibility in his generation to redeem his name by his own valor and integrity. Thus, the warrior bears his name upon his uniform.

Moreover, the warrior bears his service's name upon his uniform to honor the many warriors who fought and died under that banner. Likewise, the warrior should reflect with every action whether his actions bring honor upon the valorous warriors who fought and died before him. In this way, the warrior views himself as a re-birthing of the ancient, victorious warriors of the past. And, as he ventures to fill their shoes, he musters incredible courage to press on no matter how insurmountable the objective.

Hope

In 2 Samuel 18:24-27, David is hopeful two arriving messengers will be bearing good news from the battlefield against Absalom's rebellion. Even in the midst of war, David was diligent to maintain hope.

The importance of "hope" is vast. Whenever you are faced with a potential problem, *"planning for the worst, but hoping for the best,"* is the preferred approach. This allows you to make adequate preparation without being overcome by stress.

For example, let's say you are expecting an event to take place on July 1st. Perhaps you have a doctor's appointment on that day, or you have a court date, or you are scheduled to leave for a deployment.

As you move closer to that day, your goal should be to remain hopeful—thinking about that day in a good regard. You do not want to be consumed with stress every day leading up to July 1st. Instead, you want to be happy in your assumption of hope for something good. Then, if something bad were to happen on that day, at least you spent all days leading up to it in relative satisfaction. In other words, do not allow your lack of hope to destroy every day leading up to an event. Expect good things.

Set your hope on good things at all times. Train yourself to see something positive in all things. Even in boot camp, you can find things to look forward to. Many people have made it through difficult things by simply imagining the positive. If you are having a bad day, then focus on your next meal. Think about what you will eat for breakfast. Think intently until you convince yourself of a good thing which is just at the horizon of a new day. By doing this, you will find you can endure each difficult moment. Always look for the "light at the end of the tunnel"—and focus upon something positive when you are besieged with problems.

In an incredibly extreme scenario, like a prisoner of war situation, imagine anything you can to help you to survive. . . . Anything. . . . If you need to, imagine invisible, helpful creatures who bring you invisible food. No matter what, just keep hoping and do not give up. Keep hoping in new things and keep putting moments behind you. In this way, hope can help you survive.

Influencing Others

In 2 Samuel 7:28, the Lord makes a covenant with David—promising to raise up descendants of David as kings. Then David asks God to bless and be with his descendants.

David cared for others and desired for God to dwell with people after him. Ultimately God's covenant with David is fulfilled in the Lord Jesus.

Do not merely seek blessing in your own lifetime, or during your own time in the military. Rather, think of the impact your leadership may have upon countless generations after you—each passing on the lessons you taught to your warriors. As each person gains rank in the military, they teach those "lessons learned" from their previous leaders. So, although you may have moved on from your warrior past, be confident your past leadership may continue to bear fruit.

Moreover, the lessons you taught others in the military may serve to instruct those warriors in their own post-military ventures. In these ways you can have a "lifelong" impact on those after you, by simply focusing on being a father and brother to those who share hardship with you.

When doing leadership, think of the young man before you on a grand scale. Although he may be 20 years old, your leadership should inspire him for the rest of his life. When he is 80 he should still be telling stories to his family about how hard you were on him during his time in the military.

You never know how large an impact you may have upon the lives of those you lead. Push them hard—always. Everything matters. Make them fighters.

Although not every warrior will go to war, they will need to fight at some point in their life. So, teach them resilience. Teach them to see their limitations and drive your boot into their behinds until they push beyond them.

Who knows?

That same 20 year old man may be diagnosed with cancer ten years from now. And your pattern of pushing him now may be how he masters the self-discipline needed to beat chemotherapy.

As a leader, train people to fight. Train them to never give up or surrender—ever. If you do this properly your ghost will forever remain over their shoulder in times of trial—pushing them to keep fighting.

Don't see people as they stand today. Be a leader who absolutely transforms people at their core. Find out how their minds work and interact with each piece—building them from within.

Insults & Dissent

All leaders receive criticism. It is inevitable.
So, how should we respond to idle insults?

The Bible shows us what David did . . .

In 1 Samuel 17:28-29, David's brother, Eliab, insults him in front of other soldiers. Rather than trading childish insults with his brother, David refuses. David continues in his task of motivating the army and allowing the fire within him to build in preparation for his fight against Goliath. David was in the zone and seeing red in preparation for his fight with the giant. A powerful warrior is not distracted by mere words of lesser men. He brushes off the idle comments of his brother as he focuses on the real challenge at hand: Goliath.

In 1 Samuel 17:43, David overlooks the curses placed on him by Goliath.

In 1 Samuel 23:3-5, David overlooks the dissent of some in his own army. David is convinced God is directing him to fight the Philistines at Keilah. Although his soldiers attempt to dissuade him, David stays true to his faith. Here David's faith gives him the courage and confidence to press a successful attack upon the Philistines. At times, military leaders need to go with their gut instinct rather than conceding to dissent.

In 1 Samuel 30:6-9, David overlooks his soldiers' desire to stone him following the destruction of their army base in Ziklag. David simply prays, receives guidance from God, and then chases the Amalekite army. David does not directly interact with the mutinous comments of his soldiers. He simply continues to lead them into the next action, thereby solving their grievance without directly confronting it. This was very wise indeed, because a direct confrontation would not have been as successful.

In 2 Samuel 10:3-4, David is the subject of lies told about him by another king's officials. As a result, the other country's officials mistreat David's servants by slandering and assaulting them. David avoids further humiliation to his servants by allowing them to remain away from home until their beards are regrown. For a brief time, David overlooks the mistreatment of his servants and avoids making a hasty decision. However, after the Ammonites mobilize their army, David responds (2 Sam. 10:6-7).

In 2 Samuel 16:5-13, David overlooks the cursing of a Benjamite who walked next to David's group as he fled Absalom's rebellion. Rather than assenting to Abishai, one of his warriors who wanted to kill the Benjamite, David chose to leave the Benjamite alone. David hopes the curses of the Benjamite will inspire God's increased blessing on himself. David continued to walk as the Benjamite threw rocks and dirt at him (2 Sam. 16:13).

In 2 Samuel 19:5-7, during David's grieving for his son, Absalom, his general Joab advantageously threatens David—saying he will lead away the army from David's kingship unless he stops grieving. David complies with Joab and stops grieving. He overlooks Joab's threat rather than punishing him for it. David simply relieves Joab of his command by replacing him with Amasa (2 Sam. 19:13).

In 2 Samuel 19:22, David refuses to put a man to death who insulted and assaulted him. He stated he did not need to do so because he knew he was king. In other words, David did not need to punish people to boost his ego. His identity in God allowed him to overlook offense.

In 2 Samuel 1:17-27, David shows great tact in his mourning lament composed for the deceased King Saul and his son, Jonathan. In this lament, David makes no mention of the mistakes of the deceased king, nor how Saul mistreated him. Rather, David focuses only on positive aspects of Saul and his kingship. This is indeed graceful of David—to be wronged by Saul, yet still granting him dignity in the end.

So, when you are insulted, consider carefully how you choose to react. In many cases, choosing to overlook an offense can actually work out for greater long-term benefit. Avoid making snap decisions when responding to others. And if you do choose to respond, do so with strategy, carefully planning the scenario to come out on top and maintain your reputation. God will give you wisdom as you make these decisions.

Jobs You Don't Want

In 1 Samuel 16:21, the young David accepts his first official position as the armor bearer of King Saul.

Knights typically begin as armor bearers— learning as apprentices of the warriors who have served before them. Therefore, to be accepted as the king's armor bearer was a great honor.

In a twist of irony, it is funny David served as the armor bearer of Saul, yet when preparing to fight Goliath he refused to wear any of the armor he carried (1 Sam. 17:38-39).

Grow where you are planted . . .
Although you may be ordered to serve in a certain position you don't want, you get to choose for yourself what you will take away from it and what you will not.

When offered different roles within the military, one should see them as opportunities for professional growth. Some billets are better than others, but by having the right attitude one can benefit from any duty. Often those less desired duties can provide a warrior with opportunities to develop different skills. So, regardless where one finds himself, the goal should be to glean all potential knowledge from that duty while "stuck" there.

During David's time as the armor bearer, he decided he was not a warrior like Saul. Rather he was his own type of warrior—needing only a simple weapon and minimal gear. David's tenure as armor bearer came to an end when he was appointed as a military commander following his victory against Goliath (1 Sam. 18:13).

So, no matter how undesirable your assignment may be, remember it is temporary. Learn what you can and focus on the day when you will be re-assigned.

Labor & Officials

In 2 Samuel 8:15-18 it describes David's government organization. Under his kingship, David had an army general, a recorder, two priests, a secretary, a tabernacle official and his sons. In 2 Samuel 20:23-26 the officials of David are listed: Joab was army general, Benaiah leader of the Levites, Adoniram overseer for forced labor, Jehoshaphat was recorder, Sheva was secretary, Zadok and Abiathar over the priests, and Ira the Jairite was David's priest.

All military units need to be organized. On the smallest level it is important to divide labor and assign tasks to those on your team. Even if your team only has four people, make each person in charge of a specific task for the team.

For example, you can put one person in charge of physical fitness training for the group. Another person could be in charge of inspections for the team to ensure all people have the required gear and items for missions, overseeing the other people's barracks rooms, and so on. And another person on your four-man team could be responsible for training the others on your military occupational specialty (MOS) knowledge. Then, you as the leader would oversee each person on your team.

No matter how many people you are in charge of, you always want to divide labor and put everyone in charge of something. You goal is to make more leaders—each capable of professionally developing others. By doing this your unit will become much more proficient.

Everyone contributes to the team. Put everyone in charge of something—even if he is the most junior service-member.

Leadership from the Front

In 1 Samuel 17:26-32, David motivates Israel's terrified soldiers. Then David is the first person to step onto the battlefield. After his defeat of Goliath, the formerly terrified soldiers follow David onto the battlefield (1 Sam 17:52).

This shows the ideal style of leadership. When warriors are terrified, the leader must go before them—simply stating, *"Follow me."*

As a leader, be mindful how you present yourself before your troops. When people are fearful it shows. However, if a leader feigns confidence when they are frightened, the leader's troops will become courageous—following the leader's cue. But if the leader appears scared, then his troops will likewise become disheartened.

Strong men do not follow cowards—especially in dangerous situations. When a leader looks scared, his troops no longer trust him. This makes situations even more dangerous.

So, if you are a leader, check your fear and consider carefully how you appear to your troops. If you are scared, counteract these emotions by using intensity or scoffing. Make light of your situation in front of your troops so they do not feel intimidated by the mission. Laugh about it. Get loud and get motivated. Give your troops a motivating speech—

casting a vision within their minds of events which will take place after the mission is complete.

Need examples?

In 1 Samuel 23:3-4, David's soldiers were fearful, but his confidence and courage in the Lord's guidance inspired them to follow him. As a result, David's army was successful in rescuing Keilah from the Philistines.

Then, throughout the Bible, David continually leads his people by going before them . . .

In 1 Samuel 18:13, David steps into his anointed role as a leader similar to the Judges. He successfully leads all Israel and Judah in various military campaigns as a commander of 1,000 soldiers.

In 1 Samuel 18:30 it says David was the most successful of the military commanders.

In 1 Samuel 30:10, David leads his 400 warriors in pursuit of the Amalekite raiders.

In 2 Samuel 5:2-5, David's leadership unites the warring countries of Judah and Israel. Effective leaders can bring an end to conflict and unite different people in purpose. Following his appointment as king, David leads Israel to attack Jerusalem—establishing his new capital in that city.

In 2 Samuel 6:1-2, David assembles the army of Israel—leading them to move the ark.

In 2 Samuel 7:11, God speaks through the prophet Nathan, referring to David in the same context as the Judges—whom He raised up for specific purposes. Although David is called "king," in the grand pattern of the Bible he is fulfilling the responsibilities of a Judge.

In 2 Samuel 10:15-18, David leads Israel's army in battle against the Arameans. Even though David had mighty men capable of leadership, he chose to fight in critical battles to gain a decisive national advantage. As a result of this battle, David made the Arameans subject to Israel—likely requiring payment of tribute and putting garrisons within their territory (2 Sam. 10:19).

In 2 Samuel 12:29, after Joab and the army cut off the water supply in the siege of Rabbah, David gathers the remaining forces/people to make a final rush on the city.

In 2 Samuel 15:17-18, David leads his household and people away from Jerusalem to protect them from Absalom's rebellion.

In 2 Samuel 21:15, David led Israel in his last battle against the Philistines. David, however, became exhausted on the battlefield and was rescued from death by his bodyguard, Abishai.

In 2 Samuel 24:17, David asks God to afflict him with a plague rather than Israel. Although this may be difficult to understand, what we can learn from this is David had a desire to bear suffering on behalf of those he led.

Overall, when you lead troops, always lead from the front, or in the place where you reckon you leadership is most needed—at the point of "greatest friction." Always project courage to your troops and set aside your fear for their sake. Always appear strong and confident before your troops.

By saying "leadership from the front," I do not mean the leader must always be positioned in a direct assault group. "Leadership from the front" means the leader will always be among his people, bearing burdens with them—serving where he is needed most to direct team activity and inspire troops.

For example, consider my discussion of dividing up one's unit into three groups: direct assault, flanking and reserve. By saying "leadership from the front," this may mean you choose to place yourself within any of the three groups for a particular mission. In other words, the leader will not always be in the direct assault group. The leader would place himself at the point of "greatest friction." This means the leader may choose to fight in either the flank group or reserve group for a mission.

How would the leader determine the point of "greatest friction?"

Think about what group has the most complex mission, or the biggest chance for success, or the largest risk of failure. This is the point of greatest friction. Put yourself in whatever group you are most needed.

When should a leader place himself in the *flanking group*?

A leader should place himself in the flanking group when he wants to directly control the speed and tempo of its movement, or in cases where its secrecy might be compromised. Or if the flanking group has an inexperienced leader, you may want to be there to observe your subordinate leader—offering immediate corrective instructions to him if necessary.

When should a leader place himself in the *reserve group*?

Easy: If you expect your enemy to break contact and flee as soon as they are engaged by your direct assault group, it would make sense for you to position yourself within the reserve group. Then you can directly control the setting and execution of an ambush along the enemy's expected line of retreat.

Hopefully these examples show you clearly where you should position yourself as a leader during a combat mission. Think about the point of greatest friction, then put yourself in that group so you can best inspire and direct the actions of your troops. Take up the most difficult position and "lead from the front."

Lies, Manipulation & Slander

How to deal with manipulation . . .

Earlier in this book we discussed the importance of "distrusting" people. A person must earn your trust. Until then, suspect all people of having motives against you—especially when you are deployed and the stakes are high.

Always ask yourself, "What could this person gain for betraying me?" As you consider the answer to this question you will discover many people you encounter could in fact be attempting to manipulate or deceive you for their own purposes. Always be wary of this.

In 1 Samuel 18:22-27, the attendants of King Saul seek to manipulate David by deceiving him into thinking they all love him. King Saul uses peer pressure to manipulate the young David into mutilating the corpses of deceased Philistines. Saul has his officials command David to remove foreskins from deceased Philistines soldiers. This peer pressure is designed to influence the naïve, young David into believing this is an acceptable action.

Years later, it is likely these corpse mutilations afflicted the mind of David as he later understood the gravity of his actions. Thus, Saul uses deception and manipulation through peer pressure to intentionally damage the young mind of David— afflicting his mind with horrible memories which would stick with him forever. (In my book, <u>Dear David: Learning to See God through PTSD, Anxiety and Depression</u>, I discuss this further.)

The above is a horrible example, but it demonstrates the lengths to which others may go to harm those they dislike. In this case, Saul harbored a grudge against David, so he designed an elaborate deception by having his officials say kind things to David. Once David bought into their initial deception, the officials convinced him to do things for which he later detested himself.

In all cases, guard yourself and your heart. Do not allow yourself to be manipulated into situations. Suspect others of harboring ill intent. And, if you think it likely a person may have a hidden motive, do not allow yourself to be led into a bad situation.

How to see through deception . . .

In 2 Samuel 1:1-16, David exhibits the wisdom to see through the duplicity of a man who claims he delivered the death blow to Saul as an act of mercy. The man arrived at David's camp, in Ziklag—within Philistine territory. He claimed he fled from the battle along with the Israelites. Yet, instead of travelling in the correct direction—toward safety in Israel's territory, the man runs deep into Philistine territory. Although the text does not say, we can imagine this small detail may have clued David into the duplicity of the man. David determines he could have attempted to save Saul, rather than kill him. Therefore, David orders the man's execution.

When considering the above, it is likely the man desired to gain a reward from David for killing Saul. This would explain why the man fled from the battle in the incorrect direction. His arrival at Ziklag signals he was somehow permitted to pass through Philistine forces. The entire situation seemed fishy, and David was wise enough to see through the deception attempt.

Later, in 2 Samuel 4:5-12, David distrusts the men who murdered the king of Israel. The two men say kind words to David, as if they were friends of his kingship. David saw through their veiled wickedness—determining their action was unrighteous. He orders their execution, thus preventing the infiltration of his court with these wicked men.

Overall, remember to suspect others of deception. Think of what they would have to gain by leading you astray. Then weigh their actions accordingly to determine if they are being honest. In most cases you will find people have ulterior motives.

As a military leader you will attract duplicitous sycophants—so be wary of kind words at all times.

How to deal with lies . . .

#1 Prove it isn't true . . .

In 1 Samuel 19:17, Saul's daughter slanders David—saying he threatened to kill her. In this case, David was fleeing from King Saul, so he couldn't confront the lie. However, when David later met with Saul in the wilderness, he made it clear he had no ill intentions toward him (1 Sam. 24:14-17).

Considering the above, if someone lies about you, make it a point to correct the lie as soon as you can. Discuss your true intentions with the person.

Also, "prove" your case. Do not simply argue against the lie, but present proof to the contrary. In David's case, he "proved" he did not want to kill Saul by presenting to him a corner or his garment and a spear which he took when he infiltrated the king's camp. Thus, David proved he did not want Saul dead. Surely if he desired to harm Saul or his people, the piece of garment and the spear showed he had opportunity to do so.

How can you "prove" your case? Perhaps you can cite specific examples of your work behavior which demonstrate the lie is not true.

#2 Correct the damage caused by the lie, and ignore it . . .

Later, in 2 Samuel 10:3-4, David is the subject of lies told about him by another king's officials. As a result, the other country's officials mistreat David's servants by shaving their beards and cutting their garments.

Rather than confronting the lie, or the officials themselves, David simply chooses to correct the damage. David tells his servants to take an extended vacation until their beards grow back. It is not until the other country marches to war against David that he takes any further measures.

If you are ever in a situation where a lie is told about you, carefully weigh your options. It might be good to go with option #1 above to prove it isn't true. But in other cases it might be better for you to simply correct the damage of the lie and pretend like it didn't happen. As you make this decision, you can pray for wisdom and God will guide you.

#3 Open Door transparency . . .

Usually liars are cowards—which is why they try to hide and tell their secret tales. So, dispelling their cowardly nonsense is often quite easy. Simply consider doing one of the above two options (#1 or #2). After you do this, address your unit as a whole.

When addressing your unit, highlight the fact that liars are cowards. Stress you have an "open door" policy to discuss issues—meaning there is no legitimate reason for people to lie . . . except if they are too cowardly to openly discuss issues. Do this however you feel comfortable, fostering a candid command climate where issues are discussed openly—inviting people to come to you directly.

This will prevent future occurrences because you will be extending an open invitation to all people in your unit to discuss issues. When liars begin to spread falsehoods, members in your unit can challenge them to discuss it with you in person. If you do this you will find it will shut down much backbiting within your unit.

Mental Clarity & Prayer

Prayer gives clarity . . .

Silent reflection and contemplation can center your mind—giving clarity. When facing overwhelming circumstances, pray. Taking a moment to collect your thoughts in prayer can help you develop an action plan.

In 1 Sam. 30:6-8, David prays to find guidance after his army base in Ziklag was raided and destroyed.

Then, in 2 Samuel 21:1, David seeks God's face to determine the cause of a three year famine.

When you are stressed, avoid the temptation to charge forward. If you have time available, walk away from the problem for a while, then come back to it.

For me, physical fitness was intertwined with this process. When I felt stressed, I would go for a long run and pray—often about things which had nothing to do with my dilemma. I found my mind tended to sort its way through problems when I did this. After exercising I would gain clarity.

Mentorship & Professional Development

What is a "battle buddy?"
"Battle buddies" are two people in the military who look out for one another. There are no "lone wolves" in the military. Everyone should have a person on whom they can rely—who has their back at all times.

A battle buddy provides accountability and brotherhood . . .
An individual's first experience with the battle buddy concept will be in boot camp. When a recruit makes a mistake and is told to do push-ups, his squad leader has to do push-ups with him. This fosters accountability. When someone makes a mistake, they do not suffer alone. Rather, their buddy suffers with them. After the suffering they work together to improve—hopefully preventing the mistake from reoccurring.
Within adversity, people in the military grow close. Individuals care for one another as they care for themselves (1 Sam. 20:17). This close kinship results in a brotherhood—where individuals will endure great hardship for the sake of their fellows.

A battle buddy provides mentorship . . .

Every warrior should be involved in a mentorship process—whether by training a junior in an apprenticeship structure, or learning from a senior. These help to professionally develop the individual into a more proficient warrior.

If you are a leader with many subordinates, it should be your goal to pair up your troops in a way where they benefit the most. For example, if you have a guy who struggles with physical fitness, then you should make the most physically fit person in charge of them. This helps both individuals. The one who is physically fit can hone his ability to teach; while the one who is lacking can gain additional skills and motivation.

In 1 Samuel 18:1-4; 19:1-7 we see David and Jonathan looked after one another. Jonathan was a great choice for David because Jonathan previously led Israel's army, and David was a new army commander (1 Sam. 13:3). Moreover, Jonathan already exemplified a battle buddy system with his armor bearer—working with him on a scouting mission against the Philistines (1 Sam. 14:6-14).

Over time, Jonathan doubtlessly taught David many things about military tactics. After the death of Jonathan, David wrote a lament for him—reflecting on their close kinship in battle (2 Sam. 1:26). In a final tribute to his deceased friend, David shows kindness to Jonathan's crippled son (2 Sam. 9:1-13).

After David flees from King Saul, it appears Abiathar the priest becomes David's new battle buddy (1 Sam. 22:23). David and Abiathar are immediately bonded in grief after the deaths of the citizens of Nob. Throughout his travels, Abiathar remains close to David—offering him key advice at different times.

Unfortunately, at the end of David's reign, Abiathar betrays David after many years of faithful service (1 Kings 1:7). This betrayal is severe—cutting all the way to David's youth. The priest, Abiathar, with whom David often shares religious fellowship and prayer during his travels finally lifts up his heel against the aging king (Psa. 41:9).

In 2 Samuel 20:23-26 the officials of David are listed, with Ira the Jairite being named as David's priest. Apparently, Ira served as a battle buddy for David, similar to the former role of Abiathar the priest—offering David priestly accountability and counsel. In addition to his priestly abilities, it is possibly Ira had won valor for his military skill (see 2 Sam. 23:38). So, whereas Ira provided priestly counsel to David; David provided military instruction to Ira—enabling him to become a valorous warrior.

A battle buddy protects . . .

Whether in a foxhole or on patrol, a warrior always needs someone to watch his back. At the beginning of his military career David made the habit of surrounding himself with faithful fighters. At the beginning, his battle buddy was Jonathan. And, in 1 Samuel 20:1-42, Jonathan advocates for David to protect him from King Saul.

Later, in 1 Samuel 26:6-13, Abishai serves as the battle buddy of David—accompanying him as his body guard. During Absalom's rebellion, Abishai served as the unofficial battle buddy & bodyguard for David. In two situations where David is confronted by a Benjamite, his bodyguard Abishai is right next to him (2 Sam. 16:5-13; 19:16-23). Throughout his entire life, Abishai remained faithful to David. During David's final battle, it was Abishai who came to David's rescue—killing a Philistine giant to save the king (2 Sam. 21:17).

Although David had many battle buddies, above all he viewed the Lord Himself as his battle buddy. David sees God at his right hand and before him. Just as his other battle buddies would help him plan for missions, the Lord Himself begins to give David signals on battlefields (2 Sam. 5:23-24). And, as a part of his PTSD symptoms, David actually felt God always protecting him as an unseen refuge, fortress and stronghold (Psa. 2:12; 5:11; 7:1; 8:2; 9:9; 11:1; 14:6; 16:1; 17:7; 18:2, 30-31, 46; 19:14; 25:20;

27:1, 5; 28:1, 8; 31:1-4, 19-20; 34:8, 22; 36:7; 37:39-40; 40:2; 52:7; 55:8; 57:1; 59:1, 9, 16-17; 61:2-4; 62:2, 6-8; 64:10; 95:1; 141:8; 142:4-5; 144:1-2).

The battle buddy system makes military units stronger . . .

As his following grew, David built an entire cadre of "mighty men"—each capable of extraordinary feats and willing to give his life for David (2 Sam. 23:8-39). Whereas Saul had no champion in his army to fight for him; David gathered around himself many elite soldiers who were prepared for any military task.

It is likely the growth of David's "mighty men" could be attributed to the system of battle buddy mentorship established between Jonathan and David. As each mighty man grew in his military abilities, he would take into his service a new apprentice armor bearer. Over time, the cadre of David's mighty men continued to multiply until he had a massive group of elite warriors.

So, as you serve as a military leader, make effort to professionally develop your subordinates and teach them to do likewise. Everyone should be in charge of someone. By instilling this within your command you provide fertile soil for the development of increased skills within all your subordinates.

Mercy & Compassion

As a leader, be sure to find opportunities to offer sympathy and kindness when it is relevant.

Be kind to animals. In 1 Samuel 17:34-35, David rescues his sheep from an attacking lion and an attacking bear.

Help people who are in need when you have the power to deliver them. In 1 Samuel 23:5, David rescues Keilah from a military attack.

Although you may be a warrior, do not lose sight of the human within yourself. Find opportunities to grow your heart. Care about people in the different situations you find yourself. Although he was a fierce warrior, David found opportunities to be merciful . . .

In 1 Samuel 25:40, David extends a marriage proposal to Abigail to prevent her from the destitution often associated with widowhood in the ancient world.

In 2 Samuel 9:1-13, David shows kindness to a crippled son of his deceased friend, Jonathan. Later after Absalom's rebellion, the king extended forgiveness to Jonathan's son for his failure to support him (2 Sam. 19:24-29).

In 2 Samuel 10:1-2, David sends messengers to express sympathy to a grieving family.

In 2 Samuel 15:30-31, David wept, covered his head and walked barefoot as he fled from Absalom's rebellion. Within these actions, David demonstrates his great compassion for his son, Absalom. Although David could fight and crush the rebellion, he instead chose to flee to avoid confrontation and the likely death of his son. Instead, David prayed for God to bring peaceful resolution through bad counselors (2 Sam. 15:31). God immediately answers David's prayer by sending Hushai—whom David sends to infiltrate Absalom's council.

In 2 Samuel 16:5-13, David overlooks the cursing of a Benjamite who walked next to David's group as he fled Absalom's rebellion. Rather than assenting to Abishai, one of his warriors who wanted to kill the Benjamite, David chose to leave the Benjamite alone. David hopes the curses of the Benjamite will inspire God's increased blessing on himself. Later after David's victory against the rebellion, he promised he would not kill the Benjamite when he begged for forgiveness (2 Sam 19:16-23).

In 2 Samuel 18:5, David commands his army generals to be merciful to Absalom—even after Absalom committed treason against him.

Be ever watchful for opportunities to practice mercy—when appropriate. You can be a fierce warrior, but you must have a heart of compassion to balance yourself. Contain within yourself a mixture of both ferocity and compassion. Be wise. You will know when you should be governed by one or the other.

In other words, *"there is no greater friend and no worse enemy."*

When you are governed by compassion, you should have abundant kindness. But when you are governed by your military ferocity in times of battle, you should be abundantly violent. Make room for both compassion and ferocity within yourself. Be both a great friend and an unassailable foe.

Remember: No greater friend and no worse enemy.

Messengers & Couriers

In the ancient world, the Bible tells us messengers were often used by military leaders . . .

In 2 Samuel 2:5-7, David sends messengers to thank men who respectfully buried Saul.

In 2 Samuel 11:14-15, David sends a letter to Joab via Uriah. In the letter were instructions to orchestrate the death of Uriah. Thus, we can gather it was a standard practice within David's kingdom that messengers would courier letters unaware of their contents.

In 2 Samuel 11:18-25, we see David used battle reports from generals in the field. David provided instruction and counsel to his subordinate commanders via messengers.

In 2 Samuel 13:30-32, David received a messenger who reported the death of his son, Amnon.

In 2 Samuel 18:19-23, the general Joab uses messengers to send a battle report to King David.

Messengers can also be used as part of a plot. At one point in David's travels, he and his army camped near a large shepherd clan belonging to a man named Nabal.

In 1 Samuel 25:5-12, David sends messengers to speak with Nabal. Although it is appropriate to send messengers at times, a leader should be wary of using this in situations where a likely/potential conflict could occur. In this case it was not wise for David to use messengers. David had no contract with Nabal, and he was under no compulsion to provide food for David's army. Thus, it was not reasonable for David to send messengers to receive payment when there was no contract in place. David should have went in person to Nabal.

It is possible, however, David used this entire situation to psychologically manipulate the payment for his soldiers' services. When considering David's use of deception before King Achish and also before Ahimelech the priest, it is likely David used deception against Nabal (1 Sam. 21:2, 12-14). Why not? Suspecting he would not be paid, David could have sent messengers as a part of his plot. Once receiving the report from his messengers, David reacted in a way to force a favorable response from Nabal's clan. Of course, we cannot know for sure, but I think this is a good option when considering David's tactics and the situation presented.

In other words, it is most wise for you to always think how you can use standard procedures to your benefit. You can use messengers to maintain detachment from a situation, allowing it to develop to where you desire it to be. To do so effectively you must be sly and savvy. But if you need to do it, make sure you plan your steps carefully. The best military leaders are capable of being devious and cunning. Always think creatively and use everything to your advantage.

Motivation & Inspiration

Inspiring Others

In 1 Samuel 17:26-32, David interacts with Israelite soldiers to inspire national pride within them. Rather than being consumed with the fear sweeping across Israel's troops, David derides Goliath in discussion with other soldiers.

It takes time for their courage to build. After David defeats Goliath, however, the same terrified soldiers surge onto the battlefield to chase down the fleeing Philistines (1 Sam. 17:52). In this way, David motivated the terrified soldiers into taking bold action.

David's concern was not for his own safety. Rather it was for the hearts of his fellow soldiers. To be a good commander, the leader must be in tune with the hearts of his warriors. David's chief concern was for the army to gain courage.

Thus, the leader is ever in tune with the hearts of his troops. Leaders must be motivators—capable of inspiring others to make visions into reality. David inspires his fellow warriors by pumping them up and going ahead of them onto the battlefield.

In 1 Samuel 18:6-7, David's military successes motivate the common people to sing songs about him. This would have inspired national pride in the common people—encouraging them to be warriors like David. Thus, the warrior David is exalted by the people as their highest standard of soldierly virtue worthy of emulation.

David was a common, humble, young shepherd who demonstrated how the power of God can work through a simple person. For the common people, David was inspiring because he represented what they desired to become—simple people filled with God's power.

So, within the songs of 1 Samuel 18:6-7, we foreshadow the vast impact David will have on Bible spirituality. David's simplicity made his example attainable to the common people. Therefore, he gained popularity within Judah and Israel (1 Sam. 18:16).

Roaming Motivator

In 2 Samuel 18:24-27, we see David would use watchmen within his army headquarters. Apparently they were much more observant than the watchmen of Saul—who were permitted to fall asleep. David's roaming presence within his camp would have inspired watchmen and other soldiers to remain attentive to their assigned tasks. Perhaps David had discussions with soldiers as he roamed around the camp—likely providing them Psalms-type encouragement.

So, as you serve as a leader, look for opportunities to be with your warriors. Roam to all your watch posts and encourage your sentries. Make your rounds.

Inspiration found in History

David not only motivated the people of his time, but he motivated all the prophets who wrote in the Bible after him. Indeed, I believe David was the most influential person in the Old Testament. (For more information on how David transformed Bible spirituality by becoming the most influential person in Old Testament history, read Section 4 of my book, Dear David: Learning to See God through PTSD, Anxiety and Depression.)

If you are looking to have a long term impact upon people, embrace your experiences. Do not try to be like everyone else. Understand that although it may be difficult to see, all things in your life shape you into a unique person. And, as you accept yourself, you gain inner courage and strength to lead others.

Always reflect on the reasons why you are serving in the military. You are there to serve with honor as the representative of your family—which is why you wear your last name on your uniform. You also serve in lieu of the great warriors who fought, bled and died for your people ahead of you. Always serve with honor, bearing the torch for your generation, your family and your nation.

128

<u>Music & Dancing</u>

In 1 Samuel 16:18 it states David had ability to play stringed instruments. In fact, he played so well it soothed the emotional distress of King Saul (1 Sam. 16:23; 18:10; 19:9).

At first, musical ability may not appear a good military skill. However, the skill it takes to play an instrument could have provided a basis for the development of some other skills. For example, music could have served as a stress-reliever for David, allowing him to maintain focus on battlefields.

Moreover, musical instrument dexterity may have played a part in helping David develop slingshot precision.

Also, organization within music—requiring counts and memory to recite verses to songs—may have formed the basis of David's organizational abilities as a military commander. Thus, the young musician David would later use his musical skills of counting and memory to organize and administer his army upon battlefields.

Last, David's dancing ability was doubtlessly a part of his physical agility. In 2 Samuel 6:5, 12-14, David joins in the musical celebration during the movement of the ark. Therefore, David's musical ability, in an unlikely fashion, also enhanced his battlefield performance. When engaged in combat,

David would have had the agility to dance around his opponent. This is revealed in his ability to dodge Saul's spears (1 Sam. 19:10).

Overall, seemingly unrelated skills can enhance other abilities in unforeseen ways. It never hurts to have additional skills. So, always pursue knowledge and skill in addition to your normal military duties. Volunteer in the community. Serve people in the community by volunteering with a church. Complete college courses. Always keep learning and this will sharpen you as a warrior in many unforeseen ways.

<u>Name & Legacy</u>

In 2 Samuel 7:9, God states He will make David's name great. The name of a person should represent the quality of a person's character. Today, we should still seek to make our names great by ensuring we do nothing to tarnish our reputations. The noteworthy quality of David in this context was his simple, shepherd's heart. David was known for taking care of his nation similar to how he cared for his sheep. Likewise, our own names should leave behind a legacy to those who know us.

In 2 Samuel 12:25, David's name, which means "loved," passes to his son, Solomon, in the giving of his ceremonial name "Jedidiah"—which also means "loved."

No matter where you find yourself, friend, always remember you are responsible for making your own name honorable. When you work hard and focus on doing the right things—being honest and virtuous—those around you associate your last name with those values.

When you follow God in sincerity, living a disciplined life based on Jesus' commands, God promises to make your name great as well. I pray in all situations, you will be mindful of the fact you are creating a legacy for your own name by being a virtuous person. Although you will be tested by difficult circumstances, use hardships to show your true character as a person who stands fast in the midst of trouble. By doing so you will fulfill the legacy of the prophets who lived before you.

No Witnesses

In 1 Samuel 27:8-9, David raids various locations near Philistine territory. Following the raids, David's army plunders livestock and clothing. At each raid location David leaves no witnesses.

Although this is an extreme example in its original context, the principle remains true. Loose lips sink ships.

Speak quietly when you know your words could get you and your people in trouble. The best leaders know when to raise their voices and also when to whisper. And at times you are required to say something which straddles the gray line, speak it so softly that the other will need to lean toward you—barely hearing what you say. In that case, make sure you speak it to only *one* other—leaving no situation where there are multiple witnesses to the words you speak. This allows you to deny and step back from the words if they are discovered—leaving only a *single* witness, and never more than that. Thus you will preserve your anonymity if required to go beyond boundary.

So, if you must operate in the shadows, do so while preserving your utter anonymity. Trust no one. Whisper lightly. Leave no records. Only then are you sure to escape betrayal. Remember this.

<u>Opportunist</u>

The situations in which you will find yourself are vast. But always use the things around you to your advantage. Think creatively and use everything available to you.

In many cases your victories may depend on this type of creative thinking. Be unconventional and find a way to tip all odds in your favor.

Below there are many examples discussed where David creatively moved to find an advantage within his various situations . . .

In 1 Samuel 17:50-51, David mortally wounds Goliath with a slingshot to the forehead. Rather than turning his back and walking away, David quickly closes the distance, draws the Philistine's sword and uses it to behead the giant. By using the sword of Goliath, David ensured Goliath's defeat was complete. There would be no opportunity for the giant to awaken from a concussion.

If opportunity presents itself, the warrior must be proficient with the weapons used by his enemy. In 1 Samuel 21:8-9, the unarmed David asks for a weapon at the Lord's house.

A proficient warrior makes use of all available things on the battlefield—even using *terrain features* to his advantage.

In 1 Samuel 24:4, David opportunely sneaks up to Saul in a cave, cutting off a corner of his robe. Moreover in this situation, David's men interpret the opportune situation as an orchestration of divine will. When thinking of opportunities as a part of God's will it psychologically compels a person to take advantage of them.

In 2 Samuel 5:8, David uses the city water shafts to seize Jerusalem from the Jebusites.

A proficient warrior must seize opportunities to *gain allies*.

In 1 Samuel 25:4-5, David's army protects local shepherds while they are camping in the wilderness. At the completion of the season, David asks the owner to provide food for his army.

In 1 Samuel 25:39, David asks the wise woman, Abigail, to become his wife when he hears of her husband's death.

In 1 Samuel 30:11-16, David finds an exhausted man in the wilderness. He revives him with food. Then the man is questioned—ultimately leading David to the camp of the Amalekite army.

In 2 Samuel 2:6, David promises kindness to the men of Jabesh Gilead—who buried Saul after his death. Near the beginning of his reign, Saul rescued Jabesh Gilead from defeat (1 Sam. 11). David seeks to continue this good relationship established with the kingship of Saul. So, from the beginning of his reign as king of Judah, David associates himself with Saul to those who honored Saul.

In 2 Samuel 15:30-31, David wept, covered his head and walked barefoot as he fled from Absalom's rebellion. Within these actions, David demonstrates his great compassion for his son, Absalom. Although David could fight and crush the rebellion, he instead chose to flee to avoid confrontation and the likely death of his son. Instead, David prayed for God to bring peaceful resolution through bad counselors (2 Sam. 15:31). God immediately answers David's prayer by sending Hushai—whom David sends to infiltrate Absalom's council.

A proficient warrior makes use of opportunities to _gain provisions_. In 1 Samuel 21:3-6, David asks for the ceremonial bread in the Lord's house. He is an opportunist and seeks unconventional solutions to problems—even when it involves breaking sacred tradition.

In 2 Samuel 16:1, Ziba provides bread, raisins, figs and wine to David's people as they fled from Absalom's rebellion. Although Ziba was using this gift in an attempt to deceive David, ultimately David saw through his trickery (2 Sam. 16:3-4). In the meantime, however, David's party enjoyed the food provisions in the wilderness. When you are desperate, find food wherever you can find it (1 Sam. 21:3-4).

A proficient warrior *positions himself* in a location where he can benefit most. In 2 Samuel 2:1, God directed David to move into an opportune position where he would have increased likelihood of being selected as king after the death of Saul. David and his army move into Hebron—where he is shortly thereafter anointed as king of Judah.

In 2 Samuel 6:12, David heard the presence of the ark in the house of Obed-Edom was resulting in the Lord's blessing being poured out in that location. David moves to take advantage of this opportunity by choosing to retrieve the ark. In other words, he wanted to bring the blessings to himself rather than allowing them to remain at the house of Obed-Edom.

A proficient warrior takes advantage of the *squabbling of others*. In 2 Samuel 3:7-13, David took advantage of a disagreement between the king of Israel and Israel's top army general, Abner. When David was approached by Abner, he quickly accepted his offer to bring Israel under his kingship. To test his sincerity, David asks Abner to bring with him Michal, daughter of Saul.

Organization in Thirds & Mutual Support

In 1 Samuel 30:9, David allows 200 soldiers rest while 400 soldiers fight the Amalekites. This essentially is a division of his army into thirds—where one-third remains behind, while two-thirds go forward to battle.

Earlier in the Bible, other military leaders also used a division of three within the organization of their armies (Judg. 7:16; 1 Sam. 11:11; 13:17). Perhaps in this case, David is following an established pattern.

In 2 Samuel 18:1 during Absalom's rebellion, David appointed army "commanders over thousands" and "commanders over hundreds." Then David sends out the army under the command of three generals—Joab, Abishai, and Ittai (2 Sam. 18:2).

The principle of "three" in military units is still used to organize military units in the 21st century. . . .

For example, there are three fire teams in a squad. Then there are three squads in a platoon. There are three line platoons in a company. Then there are three line companies in a battalion.

So why is this principle of "three" used so often in military unit structures?

Dividing one's unit into three allows for leadership decentralization. If the entire unit relies solely upon one leader, then the unit is doomed if harm befalls that leader. However, if there are subordinate leaders in charge of subordinate units, then the entire unit can survive the loss of leaders. In the above example, there are leaders present at the fire team, squad, platoon, company and battalion levels. If harm befalls any leader, there are many experienced subordinate leaders who can step up and assume the fallen leader's position.

Dividing one's unit into three also allows the unit to provide respite to its warriors. Every warrior needs a break from time to time. Warriors can be injured as well. David's establishment of an equal reserve allowed injured and exhausted warriors opportunity for rest before reentry into the operational two-thirds of the unit (1 Sam. 30:21-25).

The dividing of a unit into mutually supporting parts is necessary for the overall health of the unit and its soldiers. If a military does not provide a means for injured and exhausted soldiers to repair, then they will fall off the unit's roster. Over time the entire military unit would be depleted. Thus, the dividing of a unit provides the means for a unit to make use of soldiers in recovery. Frankly, units who do not have divisions are altogether incapable of sustaining long-term continuous operations because they do not have a means of recovery built in.

Moreover, the dividing of a unit allows the commander to rotate troops into and out of combat. For example, in continuous operations a company on the battlefield should be replaced with a fresh company just out of its recovery/training cycle.

U.S. Marines refer to this as the "MEU cycle." MEU means "Marine Expeditionary Force." To simplify this process, a deploying unit goes through three phases: (1) training, (2) deployment, (3) recovery. A battalion tasked with providing one company for each MEU will always have its subordinate units in one of the three above phases. During the "training" phase, the company is doing specific tasks to prepare them for the various missions they may face. During the "deployment" phase, the company is engaged in combat and other missions. Last, the company enters the "recovery" phase—where warriors are granted leave and able to attend to personal matters. Then, the cycle repeats as this company resumes its next "training" phase.

In combat, the line company is further divided into three line platoons. This allows the company commander to commit two platoons to a battle, while holding the third platoon in reserve a short distance behind the other platoons. Then, at the decisive moment, the company commander "commits the reserve" to the battle. This allows for a concentration of combat power at a critical point thereby forcing the enemy to his culminating point. In other words, the effective company commander always holds an "ace up his sleeve." He does not show his full power on the battlefield until it is necessary to gain a decisive advantage.

Then, further throughout the unit, the platoon does the same with its three squads. And each squad does the same with its three fire teams. In this way, the principle of "three" allows commanders at all levels to conceal one-third of their combat power. In battle the enemy grows accustomed to fighting the forces who make themselves known. While, outside of their knowledge, the commander is directing the movement of a hidden force against him. It would be similar to fighting two men, then having a third man attack you from your flank.

Mutual Support & Attacking Enemies
This concept can be extended further to include "mutual support"—where two or more adjacent units support one another.

In 2 Samuel 10:11, Joab and Abishai divide Israel's army on two fronts. Depending on the development of the battle, the two armies were intended to support one another.

Why would they do this?

Sure if your unit is getting battered it helps to know your sister unit is going to provide you with some protection. But beyond this, nothing is as disconcerting to an enemy as being hit from his flanks while his sights are fixed on the unit ahead of him.

Example?

Imagine two lines of tanks advancing across a field toward one another—both lines intent on destroying the others. You might assume each tank would simply aim for the tank straight across from it. But in this assumption you would be incorrect. The best strategy would be for each tank to fire at a tank which is crosswise to its position—rather than straight across from it.

Why?

Several reasons:

(1) Firing at the flank of a tank provides you the biggest target and therefore the highest probability of scoring hits (because the side of a tank is larger than the front);

(2) It follows the simple "three" doctrine I discussed—where one unit serves as direct assault while another flanks. This concept still applies to tanks, and in the example I provided, the tank directly across from the enemy tank would be tasked with direct assault and keeping the enemy's eye fixed upon him—while apart from his knowledge, another

tank crosswise sights in and destroys him on his flank. And . . .

(3) Nothing is more disconcerting than being hit from an unknown location. It creates confusion and fear. The enemy expects the tank across from him will be shooting at him, but when he is blasted from elsewhere it immediately makes all the survivors scramble in terror—reeling to locate the source of the blast.

And in this confusion, the enemy now suspects his adversary is much larger than he can see—and this is a frightening possibility. The enemy may think the hit came from artillery or air support—and in that case the hidden flanking attack may compel the enemy to poop his pants.

So, in all cases, determine how adjacent units should support one another to make the most effective shots and cause the most confusion among the enemy. Divide your unit into three and make a good plan. This is how effective leaders plan for battles.

Peaceful Resolution (if possible)

In 2 Samuel 15:30-31, David wept, covered his head and walked barefoot as he fled from Absalom's rebellion. Within these actions, David demonstrates his great compassion for his son, Absalom. Although David could fight and crush the rebellion, he instead chose to flee to avoid confrontation and the likely death of his son. Instead, David prayed for God to bring peaceful resolution through bad counselors (2 Sam. 15:31). God immediately answers David's prayer by sending Hushai—whom David sends to infiltrate Absalom's council.

In all cases, attempt peaceful resolution with people. The application of deadly force should be a last option—when all other solutions would be ineffective. Taking life is permanent, so if you are in a position to make that choice do so only as a last option.

However, if deadly force "must" be used—let it be ferocious and decisive.

Perception & Walking by Faith (2 Cor. 5:7)

In 1 Samuel 17:33-34, King Saul rejects David and doubts his ability to fight Goliath. David is not swayed. Rather than judging circumstances based on physical circumstances, David sees deeper—much deeper.

David's perception allows him to see beyond Goliath's size, realizing the decisive battlefield factor will be God. To David, Goliath's size is a non-factor. Earlier as a shepherd, David killed both a lion and a bear—getting close enough to grab their hair before delivering the coup de grace.

David was not a mere *physical* warrior. Although he possessed physical strength and ability, his decisive ability was his *supernatural perception*. David's faith was so strong it energized him with courage—allowing him to transport incredible power from the spiritual realm to his present circumstances.

Need proof?

In Ezekiel 1, we see a vision of God's heavenly kingdom suspended above the prophet. God's presence appears atop a massive angelic machine in the sky. Likewise, David viewed God's presence as a vast fortress which provided angelic power to completely transform the world around him. This is apparent throughout David's many psalms (Psa. 2:12; 5:11; 7:1; 8:2; 9:9; 11:1; 14:6; 16:1; 17:7; 18:2,

30-31, 46; 19:14; 25:20; 27:1, 5; 28:1, 8; 31:1-4, 19-20; 34:8, 22; 36:7; 37:39-40; 40:2; 52:7; 55:8; 57:1; 59:1, 9, 16-17; 61:2-4; 62:2, 6-8; 64:10; 95:1; 141:8; 142:4-5; 144:1-2).

This heavenly fortress/refuge/stronghold followed David throughout all his journeys—ensuring he was never alone or unprotected in the wilderness.

As a physical warrior, David was *intimidating*. However, as a spiritual warrior, David was *immortal*—his supernatural perception allowing him to visualize all the powers of heaven bearing down on the land around him. This supernatural perception provided an inexhaustible source of courage, strength, confidence and skills—tilting all battles in David's favor. David did not trust in physical fortresses—being at peace most in the wilderness where he was solely protected by the supernatural fortress of God (Psa. 23). David's fortress was supernatural and moved with him.

However, later within his *physical* Zion fortress, David shifted to his role as a religious leader for the Israelites. In 2 Samuel 5:10, it states God was with David. As a result he kept growing more and more powerful. It is likely he penned many of his psalms during this time—reflecting on his past experiences. Thus, David's power was supernatural and spiritual. He grew in power as he led Israel further through his writing and teaching.

David had spiritual perception. He heard the voice of God and saw His activity in the world around him.

In 2 Samuel 5:19-20, David prays and God directs him to attack the Philistine army at Baal Perazim. Following this battle, God gives David specific instructions on how to successfully attack the Philistines in the Valley of Rephaim (2 Sam. 5:22-24). In this case, David hears the sound of supernatural "marching" in the tops of the balsam trees as the spiritual army of the Lord went ahead of David into battle.

(If you would like to learn more about how to develop this supernatural perception, see my discussion of "derealization" in my book, <u>Dear David: Learning to See God through PTSD, Anxiety and Depression</u>.)

<u>Physical Endurance & Mental Resilience</u>

In the military one must develop the ability to endure long term. It is not enough to be strong for a single day. A warrior must be physically disciplined—able to push himself beyond his limitations. When pressed, the resilient warrior is the one who will succeed.

In 1 Samuel 30:17, David and his army battle the Amalekite army for an entire night and a day. This is remarkable when considering this battle occurred at the end of four day journey (1 Sam. 30:1).

David also exemplified remarkable endurance in eluding capture by Saul for many years.

So what is the best way to develop endurance? . . .

Physical endurance is relatively easy. Simply play sports and exercise to develop your cardiovascular strength. Eventually you want to become as proficient at running as a soccer player. You should be able to run all day, every day. This will give you the physical endurance you need to fight in combat.

Mental resilience & the chow-to-chow mentality . . .

Mental resilience is a little trickier, but you can gain it through a piece-by-piece perspective. This begins in boot camp.

No matter how difficult things seem in boot camp, you can always depend on getting to eat meals. So, when you are having a tough day, think about your next meal—what they will be serving. Trick yourself into looking forward to each meal. This will help you to get through each day one step at a time. Eventually all the days add up, and before you realize it you are graduating from boot camp.

Following boot camp, continue to build your mental resilience through this piece-by-piece perspective. A memorable way to remember this . . .

> *How do you eat an elephant?*
> *One bite at a time.*

No matter how difficult or large the challenge you face, remember to confront it one step at a time. Simply focus on each "spoonful" and before you realize it, the entire elephant is eaten.

Always find something to look forward to. By seeing in your mind the "light at the end of the tunnel" you can continue to endure—no matter how difficult.

Planning & Advisers

In the U.S. Marines, military operations are planned using five parts: Situation, Mission, Execution, Administration/Logistics, and Command/Signal. This is remembered using the acronym: SMEAC.

In 1 Samuel 20, we see the operation planned by David and Jonathan adheres to this basic format . . .

Situation: David needs to determine if King Saul intends to kill him.

Mission: Jonathan tasked to determine Saul's intentions.

Execution: Jonathan and David decide on the methods used by Jonathan.

Administration/Logistics: David and Jonathan decide on the rally point, and also the location where David will hide.

Command/Signal: David and Jonathan develop a method of coded communication using arrows to convey specific messages.

Regardless of the exact planning method used by David, it is clear he made clear, careful decisions. David examined problems from multiple angles. This is similar to the method used by U.S. Marines.

So, regardless of how you plan as a military leader, be sure to use a mental checklist of some sort to ensure you leave no rock unturned.

Consult with Advisers

In the Bible, David often prayed with his prophet or priest—thereby gaining clear guidance on his next steps.

So, in cases where we are unsure of our next step, it is indeed wise to consult with a person who can likewise pray with us as we develop a good plan. At times a small bit of advice many be exactly what we need. Be mindful of this.

As you plan missions with your advisers, be open to the possibility there may be a decisive solution available if you creatively approach problems from every possible angle. For example, in 2 Samuel 5:8, David uses the city water shafts to seize Jerusalem from the Jebusites. In this way he avoids use of an extended siege through the use of an unconventional solution.

When consulting with advisers seek potential unconventional solutions. But, when you seek an unconventional solution ensure you have all your bases covered so you are not doing something which will come back to bite you. This is very important.

Example?

A vehicle maintenance section which is short on parts may think of a short term solution to take parts off of other vehicles which are broken down to use on another vehicle. However, this "unconventional solution" would come back to bite the mechanics—to the point they would probably be fired. Taking parts off vehicles to use in other vehicles is called "cannibalizing" and it is a big no-no.

When seeking unconventional solutions, just remember to be smart. Think about where you are and what you must do. And be careful to consider your options so you do not suffer negative after-effects.

In cases where you are required to do things which might be scrutinized it is best to ensure your directions are not public knowledge. In those cases, see the section "*No Witnesses.*" Frankly you should not trust people, so loose lips are a definite limiting factor on your decision-making.

Those who do not show careful discretion eventually get burned. Bean counters are constantly running numbers and taking inventories, so people who use unwise shortcuts are eventually run ashore.

Plots & Betrayal

Surviving plots . . .

In 1 Samuel 18:17-27, King Saul plotted against David by ordering him into dangerous situations intending to kill him.

Then, in 1 Samuel 19:10-11, King Saul sends officials to David's house to kill him. David narrowly escapes after being warned of the plot.

Following this event, King Saul continues to pursue David (1 Sam. 19:20).

Although David was hunted, he kept moving, stayed true to his calling from God, and he survived.

When others are plotting against you, keep moving. Stay faithful to your calling and do not let the actions of others dissuade you from the course God has assigned to you.

God has a purpose for you. Believe that. Others may dislike you, but you are not called to be liked by everyone. Just focus on doing the right things. Keep moving to safe locations and make spiritual progress however you can.

Surviving betrayal . . .

In 1 Samuel 23:8, the army of Israel pursues David. Considering David led Israel in previous battles, their willingness to hunt David under the leadership of Saul is a great betrayal. So, David was not only betrayed by single people; rather he was betrayed and rejected by an entire country (1 Sam. 24:2; 2 Sam. 15:13; 20:2). This makes David a fitting picture of Christ—who was also betrayed by the entire country (John 19:15).

Then, in 1 Samuel 23:19-24, the Ziphites betray David. They contact King Saul—informing him of David's location. Similar incidents occur in 1 Samuel 24:1 and 26:1. Indeed, it is remarkable considering the numerous betrayals endured by David that he would still desire to be king over these treacherous people.

Later, in 1 Samuel 30:6, David is nearly stoned by his army men following the Amalekite raid of his army's base in Ziklag. Rather than focusing on their threats, David prayed—receiving guidance from the Lord.

In 2 Samuel 15, David endures Absalom's rebellion and its mass betrayals which compelled him to flee from Jerusalem.

Immediately after the end of Absalom's rebellion, Israel rebelled against David again by following Sheba, son of Bikri (2 Sam. 20:1-22).

Overall, David's life was marked with many betrayals. To stay faithful in the midst of hardship, David prayed—providing him clarity and direction within the messes inflicted upon him.

So, when you are betrayed, take heart! You can survive. Pray. Work your way through the problem one step at a time. Stay true to your calling in God. And keep moving forward.

Plunder

Many armies have restrictions which ban soldiers from taking items in war. But, for the sake of discussion, I provide notes below detailing how David took plunder in the ancient world. Who knows? One day you might find yourself in a situation where this applies . . .

In 1 Samuel 17:54, David seizes the weapons and head of Goliath following the champion battle.

In 1 Samuel 23:5, David defeats the Philistines and takes their livestock.

In 1 Samuel 27:8-9, David raids various locations near Philistine territory. Following the raids, David's army plunders livestock and clothing.

In 1 Samuel 30:18, David's army plunders the Amalekite raiders—taking livestock and their families who were kidnapped from Ziklag. David uses some of the extra plunder to send gifts to the elders of Judah (1 Sam. 30:26-31). Three days after David's return to Ziklag, he learns of the deaths of Saul and Jonathan (2 Sam. 1:1-2). So, the plunder gifts sent to the elders of Judah served a purpose in prompting David's imminent appointment as the king of Judah (2 Sam. 2:4).

In 2 Samuel 5:21, David's army destroys idols left behind by the Philistine army.

In 2 Samuel 8:7-8, David plunders gold and bronze from the Arameans after defeating them in battle.

In 2 Samuel 8:11-12, David dedicates war plunder to the Lord's house—including gold, silver and bronze.

In 2 Samuel 12:30, David plunders gold from the Ammonite city, Rabbah.

Poise

Poise is the ability to stand under pressure. A football quarterback must stand patiently, while defenders bear down upon his position—waiting for just the right moment to throw the football.

In 1 Samuel 30:6, David is nearly stoned by his army men following the Amalekite raid of his army's base in Ziklag. Rather than focusing on their threats, David prayed—receiving guidance from the Lord (1 Sam. 30:8).

Rather than David crumbling under the pressure of threats and plots against him, David stands fast in the Lord. He prays with his prophet, waiting for the right guidance to arrive from God. Thus, David exemplifies great poise under pressure.

In the military you may find yourself in similarly difficult situations. And in those situations, stand fast under pressure. Perform to the best of your ability. Press forward.

Predict Human Behavior

To be a proficient military leader, one must develop the ability to understand people. You must guess what people are thinking. By doing so, you can determine how they will approach certain situations.

Why is this important?

Understanding your enemy allows you to accurately predict their next actions. Then you can position yourself to exploit an advantage. In other words, if you can predict where an enemy will hit, you can remove yourself from that location and intercept his attack with a decisive counter-attack.

Understanding your leaders allows you to act on "commander's intent"—especially in their absence.

Understanding civilians and those who work with your unit while deployed will allow you to see who has motives to betray you.

And understanding your own subordinates allows you to look out for their personal interests. By looking out for your warriors you can further gain their "trust and confidence"—making them more loyal fighters for you.

In the Bible, David exemplifies these types of human understanding. He often used his human understanding to guess the motives of those around him. This allowed him to remain guarded against potential threats.

In 1 Samuel 20:3, David perceives Saul's motive for hiding his plot from Jonathan. This shows David developed the ability to view situations from other people's perspectives—even when Jonathan was not capable of doing so (1 Sam. 20:2).

In 1 Samuel 20:7, David predicts the two potential responses of King Saul to Jonathan when he reports David's absence. This means David was perceptive in his understanding of people—predicting their actions and the potential ways they could affect him. Then David would plan his response to multiple potential scenarios. Remember this method and put it into practice.

As a commander, David used his ability to predict human behavior to anticipate enemy actions. In 1 Samuel 27:1-2, David moves out of Israelite territory into the land of the Philistines. As David predicts, Saul abandons pursuing David (1 Sam. 27:4).

In 1 Samuel 27:8-12, David effectively uses deception against King Achish for one year and four months. While living in Philistine territory outside the reach of King Saul, David continues to fight for

Israel. David leads his army in raids against Israel's enemies near and within Philistine territory.

However, when David gives battle reports to King Achish, he falsely reports raids against Israel and her allies. And David leaves no one alive to report contrary to his words. Thus, David lives under the jurisdiction of the Philistine king while still fighting for Israel. David predicts the actions of King Achish and likely informants, and cleverly devises a raiding method to address various contingencies.

In 2 Samuel 1:1-16, David exhibits the wisdom to see through the duplicity of a man who claims he delivered the death blow to Saul as an act of mercy. The man arrived at David's camp, in Ziklag—within Philistine territory. He claimed he fled from the battle along with the Israelites. Yet, instead of travelling in the correct direction—toward safety in Israel's territory, the man ran deep into Philistine territory. Although the text does not say, we can imagine this small detail may have clued David into the duplicity of the man. David determines he could have attempted to save Saul, rather than kill him. Therefore, David orders the man's execution.

In 2 Samuel 1:20, David predicts the Philistines will rejoice when they hear of Saul's death. This reveals David's knack for predicting the secondary effects of certain actions. This was a part of his PTSD hypervigilance—where he would constantly think about how actions would affect further actions, and how he could prepare for each emerging contingency. Thus, before the Philistines could even receive a report of Saul's death, David already considered what they would do in response—and how this would impact his own future. In his mind David ever remained steps ahead of his enemies as a result of his PTSD hypervigilance. (For more information on this topic, read my book: <u>Dear David: Learning to See God through PTSD, Anxiety and Depression</u>.)

In 2 Samuel 4:5-12, David distrusts the men who murdered the king of Israel. The two men say kind words to David, as if they were friends of his kingship. David saw through their veiled wickedness—determining their action was unrighteous. He orders their execution, thus preventing the infiltration of his court with these wicked men.

In 2 Samuel 14:19, David sees through a ruse presented by Joab—recognizing he had motive to send a woman to his court to garner sympathy for David's banished son, Absalom.

In 2 Samuel 15:14, David flees his palace when he predicts the arrival of Absalom's rebellion.

So, in all cases it helps to think ahead. In the military, always work to predict the actions of others. Understand their perspectives and plan accordingly so you are never taken by surprise. Understand the reasons why a person may make certain decisions, and position yourself in a way to maintain an advantage regardless of the decision they may make. Think about different scenarios, and have a counter action planned for each one.

In other words, this is how you should constantly think . . .

"*When this happens, it is likely this person will do* _____, *because* _____."

"*Or they could* _____."

"*If they do* _____, *then I will* _____."

"*Or if they do* _____, *then I will* _____."

Is this type of hypervigilance exhausting? Absolutely. But your survival depends upon it. If you are in a dangerous place, you must have the ability to think ahead—exhausting different scenarios to ensure you and your warriors are trained and prepared for all possible "what if" scenarios.

This is the responsibility of a good leader. Think carefully through all potential problems and find solutions for *everything*. This allows you to rapidly match contingencies with ready responses. This is the behavior of a proper leader—who maintains control and poise in the midst of chaos. This is how it is done.

Remarkably, those with PTSD are more adept at this type of thinking. Hypervigilance brings about this type of beneficial thinking naturally. So, if you have been through tough times you may be graced with an increased ability to plan and respond to dangerous situations. Do not shy away from this ability if you have developed it. Use it to your advantage. PTSD can actually save your life.

You should be so hypervigilant you can feel events before they happen. And at that moment you have a surge within yourself, drawing you to a particular thought, it is then you act quickly and decisively. This is how you survive.

Feel everything around you, drawing in a picture of your surroundings with every breath. There is a reason why those practiced in martial arts stress a connection to the environment around them. If you are sufficiently hypervigilant your feet should allow you to feel everything around you. You should walk by faith, not by sight—seeing far more with your mind than you do with your eyes.

Remember this and put it into practice. God will give you the wisdom and knowledge you need to direct things around you.

You are in control of your surroundings, so move like a person who is in control.

Think like a person who is in control.

Take charge of everything around you in your battlespace and move it to your advantage. You are not a mere thing in your environment—like other passive people and things; you are in charge of what happens around you. So move things—with your mind, with your voice, with your body. This is how you use hypervigilance to your advantage.

Pride & Desired Outcome

Over time warriors can develop pride. Pride can be good because it lends confidence and courage. But, pride can be bad if it is not used for a good, inspirational purpose. Pride can be detrimental if a person lacks level-headed wisdom.

In the following confrontation, David demonstrates how to properly balance pride and wisdom . . .

In 2 Samuel 19:22, David refuses to put a man to death who insulted and assaulted him. He stated he did not need to do so because he knew he was king. In other words, David did not need to punish people to boost his ego. His identity in God allowed him to overlook idle offenses.

This account is interesting because David demonstrates superior moxie by doing nothing to the offender. Think about it this way . . .

If David would have executed the man, then others would have thought, "Wow, David has the authority and power to execute people."

But ultimately that is a fruitless accomplishment for him to convince people of that. Of course everyone knew David could choose to execute people. So, what is the point in executing someone who is truly harmless?

However, David chose to reply in a way which completely humiliated the man—treating him as if he were altogether insignificant. In other words, David used the man to prop himself up as he verbally brushed him aside.

In this case, David's approach was superb. He avoided bloodshed while making himself look even more powerful to the people. And, while doing this he references the fact he is king. In this David shows he is not an insecure man who has something to prove. He shows himself to be a great king who cannot waste his time with the idle musings of lesser, cowardly men.

In your leadership, do likewise. If someone trifles with you, show him by your words how truly insignificant he is. And when he is humiliated by your well-placed response it will dissuade others from attempting to insult you.

When you are moved to a defensive position against someone else, always ask yourself what you are looking to accomplish with your words. Ask yourself, "What is my desired outcome?" Then use your words to bring about that outcome.

Promises & Pledges

Promises . . .

When making allies/friends, it is necessary to establish a "give and take" in your relationship. You should help them just as they help you.

When deployed you may have to rely upon other people outside of your unit. So every time you can, help out other people and ask them to help you.

There are several examples where David makes promises to other people. . . .

In 1 Samuel 24:21-22, David swears by oath not to wipe out all Saul's descendants.

In 2 Samuel 5:3, David makes a covenant with Israel when he is anointed as their king.

In 2 Samuel 14:11, David gives an oath in the name of the Lord to protect one of his citizens from avengers.

In 2 Samuel 19:13, David gives an oath in the name of the Lord as he appoints Amasa as his army general, replacing Joab.

In 2 Samuel 19:23, David gives an oath in the name of the Lord that he would not put Shimei to death for cursing him and throwing rocks and dirt at him.

Pledges and promises to subordinates . . .

As a military leader, it is important to put things into writing so they cannot be altered. If you are providing guidance, and if it is appropriate to put it in a written counseling, do so. This ensures both you and the other party to remain faithful to the agreement.

Be true to your pledges. Your word is your honor. Do what you say you will—especially in cases where if you fail to follow through it will result in a marring of your appearance before troops. When you pledge something, you must be sure to deliver, so in the future when you speak your troops will heed every word.

If you say you will do something, you should do it—as a general practice. This accustoms your troops to the fact that you always follow through. And, in cases where you need to compel troops to carry out a certain action or meet a deadline, if you threaten them they will be sure to act with diligence on the threat.

If however you choose to later withdraw the threat, you must feign reluctance—stressing you are going outside of what you normally do. This allows you to maintain your reputation as a leader who follows through, but rewards troops with grace when they perform exceptionally.

In other words, always be mindful of how your actions will cause you to be perceived in the eyes of your people. To lead warriors in combat you must appear like a god walking among mortals, and you must cause yourself to be revered in the eyes of those you lead. Strong men will not follow weak men.

For more information on how to discipline your self-image as a leader, read <u>The Mask of Command</u> by John Keegan.

Promotions & Billets

In the military, promotions to higher ranks are often sought by warriors, so please allow me to share some of my reflections . . .

Over time, you may be assigned to certain jobs you enjoy, and at other times you may feel lost within your circumstances—just counting the days until you can leave.

If indeed you ever find a job in the military you enjoy, it is worth holding onto. Many times people seek promotions. And when they are promoted quickly they may be placed in a new position where they have no peace and are constantly afflicted with unnecessary stress.

So, when thinking about your career, I counsel you to consider remaining in a job where you are happy, rather than chasing green grass. If you find yourself in a position where you are making a positive contribution and for which you feel uniquely capable, do not be hasty in seeking a promotion which will compel you to leave your good calling.

Throughout David's lifetime as a warrior, we see he served in many different locations, in many different billets. But near the end of his life, he mused on the simplicity he always desired—saying he wanted only to dwell in the Lord's house (Psa. 27:4). In other words, David matured to the point where he realized a simple life of honoring God was much more desirable than all the glory which was accorded to those who chased after fame.

And, more interesting, there are two people in David's life whose names mean "fame"—David's brother Shimeah, whose descendant caused contention, and the Benjamite Shimei who threw stones at David (2 Sam. 13:3 & 16:13).

So, there is a lesson here—if you choose to chase "fame" and promotions the end result will be contention and targeting. When we seek to stand atop a pedestal, it becomes more likely others will seek to knock us down.

So, if you seek promotions, you do well. But be wary of increased problems which often accompany them. While serving at lower ranks your peers actually look out for you and are concerned for your success. But at the highest ranks in the military there is tight competition—where your peers will step on you and bad-mouth you to get the next promotion or higher billet ahead of you. So, the further you go in ranks, the less people you have who are truly concerned for you. And the brotherhood associated with the lower ranks is replaced by a brood of sycophants who begin to gather around you.

Serve with honor and distinction in the military, but do not push yourself unnecessarily to your detriment. Consider what you want and pursue it with diligence. And if at any point you desire to slow your promotions or billet-seeking, carefully weigh the "pro's and con's" of your choice.

Is the added stress worth the extra pay? You must decide for yourself.

Prophetic Leaders & Advisers

In the military leaders rely on subject matter experts (also called SMEs). A SME is a person who is especially knowledgeable in a particular subject.

In your military travels, gather around you capable people who can assist you in your missions. When making decisions, ask these specialists for their counsel, then make decisions based on all the information you receive.

Prophetic Advisers

In the Bible, the warrior-leader David received counsel from his priests and prophets—who served as his advisers. These priests and prophets would pray with David, helping him to think deeply about his situation so he could make good decisions.

In 1 Samuel 22:5, David listens to the counsel of his prophet, Gad. Here he warns David about the risks of staying in the Moabite stronghold. Prophets were known for their ability to "see" the future. Thus, the warning from the prophet indicates something negative may have happened if David stayed in the stronghold. He would have been vulnerable to capture similar to the event where he was brought before King Achish in 1 Samuel 21.

In 1 Samuel 25:30, Abigail offers a prophecy of David's future—where he will be appointed ruler of Israel. David listens to the counsel of Abigail, similar to how he listens to the counsel of Gad.

As a military leader, make sure you have wise advisors with the ability to "see" the potentially negative outcome of actions. By doing so, you can prevent yourself from being put in positions where you experience loss. Although your SMEs might not be "prophets," they should have the uncanny ability to predict outcomes from basic cause-effect situations—warning you to take specific actions to best safeguard your unit and ensure success.

In 1 Samuel 23:16-18, Jonathan encourages David by telling him about his future. Although Jonathan was not designated a prophet, in this passage he prophesies David's future.

Prophecy is encouraging because it provides a mental anchoring point in the midst of an uncertain future. As David fled from Saul his entire life seemed in flux. The prophecy of Jonathan allows David to see the light at the end of the tunnel. Ultimately he will be completely delivered and blessed. Later Saul himself gives David a positive prophecy which is remarkably similar (1 Sam. 24:20).

In 1 Samuel 30:1-8, after the Amalekites raid David's military base in Ziklag, and the mutiny of his soldiers, David prays. David calls for his priest, Abiathar, and the sacred ephod. Then he receives guidance from the Lord.

In 2 Samuel 7:1-3, David consults with Nathan the prophet before beginning to construct the Lord's house.

In 2 Samuel 12:1-15, the prophet Nathan indirectly confronts King David concerning his sin against Uriah.

Anyone can be a prophetic leader. Although you have not been designated as a "prophet," you can still be a "prophetic leader." Just as Jonathan gave David a positive mental image of the future at a low point in his life, so also you can give positive mental images of the future to your warriors.

At low points, discuss with your people what they plan to do after they are delivered from their present hardship. This type of prophetic leadership helps people to get through tough times by focusing on the light at the end of the tunnel.

Moreover, military planning requires leaders to predict future events. In other words, a leader must be capable of foreseeing the potential actions his enemy will take if pressed in a certain way. So, leadership on a basic level *always* requires an element of foretelling, prediction and planning to intercept future actions.

So, just as David surrounded himself with prophets, you should still surround yourself with prophetic advisers—people with a knack for preparation based on prediction. Be a prophetic leader, and surround yourself with prophetic advisers.

God Speaking through Prophets/Priests

Just as the Bible passages below indicate, God often speaks through people. . . .

In 2 Samuel 2:1, God directed David to move into an opportune position where he would have increased likelihood of being selected as king after the death of Saul. David and his army move to Hebron—where he is shortly thereafter anointed as king of Judah.

In 2 Samuel 5:19-20, David inquires and prays for military guidance. God directs him to attack the Philistine army at Baal Perazim. Following this battle, God gives David specific instructions on how to successfully attack the Philistines in the Valley of Rephaim (2 Sam. 5:22-24).

In 2 Samuel 21:1, David prayed to seek God's counsel concerning a three year famine. God heard his prayer and granted him an answer—most likely through David's priest or prophet.

In 2 Samuel 24:10-14, David is conscience-stricken after taking the census of Israel. He prays and asks God for forgiveness. God sends Gad the prophet to David with an answer. At the end of the plague, the prophet Gad tells David to build an altar to the Lord for sacrifices (2 Sam. 24:18-19).

Mighty Men & Officials

As one gets promoted in the military, he must transition out of his previous billet. For the leader, he must give his attention to overseeing the actions of subordinates, rather than doing the work himself. Frankly, it is not possible for the leader to do everything himself, so he must delegate to subordinates and supervise them in the accomplishment of activities.

This was an area in which David was especially adept. Whereas King Saul had no champion who would fight Goliath for him; David in his kingship was surrounded by many mighty men— each willing and capable of fighting battles for him (2 Sam. 23:8-39).

And, when David appointed people to his court, he was careful to consider their advice . . .

In 2 Samuel 18:3-4, David was dissuaded from leading his army by his three generals—Joab, Abishai and Ittai. If they did not dissuade him, it is likely David would have led his army to confront Absalom's rebellion.

Later, in 2 Samuel 20:23-26 the officials of David are listed: Joab was army general, Benaiah leader of the Levites, Adoniram overseer for forced labor, Jehoshaphat was recorder, Sheva was secretary, Zadok and Abiathar over the priests, and Ira the Jairite was David's priest. Apparently, Ira served as a battle buddy for David—offering him priestly accountability and counsel.

It is possible Ira was a mighty warrior of David who also served as his priest (see 2 Sam. 23:38). So, just as David was a well-rounded warrior, who was both spiritually and physically proficient, his example encouraged others to likewise merge within themselves both faith and physical strength.

So, as you obtain promotions and increased responsibilities in the military, always give your attention to the professional development of your subordinates. Train them to be proficient, valorous warriors. Give them responsibility and put them in charge of training new warriors—thereby passing on to all members in your unit the same tenacity.

Quickness & Holy Spirit Indwelling

In 1 Samuel 17:48 it says David ran quickly. Considering other passages which note the agility of David, it is likely David was very fast (1 Sam. 18:10-11). This would have contributed to his elusiveness on the battlefield. It may have also contributed to David's stealth—allowing him to close distances in quiet environments undetected (1 Sam. 24:4).

When considering David's PTSD symptoms of depersonalization and derealization, it is interesting to ponder how he would have perceived his own movement. At times David views God as fighting battles through and from within his own body—conflating his own physical actions with the actions of God Himself. Within the mind of David, his running, walking and other movements would be likewise affected by his depersonalization.

So from David's perspective, when running forward, his mind would have toggled in and out of depersonalization—giving him the perception of gaps. And when realizing additional distance was covered during his gap in consciousness, David would have been convinced God was "running" or moving within him—taking over his body during those gaps in consciousness.

How can we understand this?

When driving it is common for drivers to lose track of their surroundings—forgetting roads, losing track of their highway exit and so on. When considering how we may have experienced this in driving, it may help us to understand how David may have felt within his own body due to his PTSD depersonalization.

David would perform physical tasks, and due to the mental gaps of depersonalization, he would have been impressed by his own ability. His running would be perceived by his mind as surges of power. He would perceive his own movement as hairpin precision—allowing him to dodge spears (1 Sam. 18:10-11).

In Psalm 18:34, David attributes his bending of a bow to both himself and the Lord. As David begins pulling the bow, he experiences a conscious gap as a result of PTSD depersonalization. Within the split second, his consciousness reemerges to find the bow bent further than his mind predicted. Thus, David interprets this as the Lord pulling the bow within him during his conscious gap.

Whereas people are prone to view PTSD as a disability, the fact is PTSD is a powerful enhancement for a warrior. The shifts in consciousness afforded by PTSD depersonalization give the warrior confidence. Rather than viewing himself as a solo warrior, David develops a view of himself as a man who is inwardly enhanced by the presence of God—empowered by the Spirit of God within him. This is a result of PTSD depersonalization.

In all cases, when David moves or performs actions, his PTSD mind would constantly support his belief that God was moving in him (through consciousness gaps).

When understanding this concept, it makes sense of the "indwelling of the Holy Spirit" in both the Old Testament and New Testament. It can be explained simply when understanding the intersection of trauma and faith—particularly how one with PTSD depersonalization can develop a remarkably personal spiritual self-perception.

So, how does this apply to you as a warrior?

Many warriors develop PTSD. Although this may create struggles in some areas of your life, your PTSD symptoms are a testament to your ability to *survive*. In my book, <u>Dear David: Learning to See God through PTSD, Anxiety and Depression</u>, I present a clear case that PTSD can greatly enhance a person's spirituality—just as it helped David.

One must simply accept and come to peace with who they are. Don't be like everyone else. Embrace your experiences and allow yourself to flourish within the boundaries God has granted you. As a person does this, he begins to feel the movements of God within and around him.

If you want to move with supernatural power, let go of the labels placed on you by "normal" people in society. Who cares what they think anyway? Realize no matter what you have been through, those past experiences grant you powerful inward gifts and abilities. By embracing who you have become you can develop the ability to see what others cannot see and experience what "normal" people cannot.

The Bible is a spiritual book based on the survival of ancient people—especially the Lord Jesus, who endured fasting and affliction throughout His earthly life, culminating in His brutal death upon the cross.

Consider this carefully: *You do not want to be a normal person.* You want to follow in the footsteps of Christ—living a disciplined life, ever growing in your ability to gain victory over hardships. And, as you realize this one thing, you come to the powerful realization that the Bible was written about and by survivors like you—who were also rejected by "normal" society.

If you desire supernatural power as a warrior, let go of society's definitions of "normal." Embrace the rocky, uphill path God has assigned to you. Discipline yourself upon it—and within your discipline you will experience God moving and directing your steps, empowering every footfall with divine power sending shockwaves around you (1 Cor. 9:24-27). When you walk you will move forward in surges—feeling electricity moving in surges and waves around you. This is how you must enter your battlefields.

<u>Raids</u>

Raids are military operations where you attack an enemy at a certain location, then quickly leave the location.

In 1 Samuel 27:8-9, David raids various locations near Philistine territory. Following the raids, David's army plunders livestock and clothing.

Then, in 1 Samuel 30:15-18, David and his army of 400 raid the Amalekite army camp.

People may have the incorrect assumption when you fight an enemy you stay in the same location where you defeated him—making that location your new territory. This is false.

Depending on your situation, after defeating an enemy you may need to move out of the location rapidly to avoid counterattack. If you stay in the same location the enemy from another location may be moving to attack you. So, by moving out of that location they lose track of you. And by doing so, you safeguard your unit.

Rally Points & Contingency Plans

Murphy's Law tells us to expect problems—with everything. So, during your military operations, always have contingency plans. Rehearse them if possible. That way when things go south your unit will be somewhat prepared.

In the Bible, the warrior David used rally points as a part of his military planning. . . .

In 1 Samuel 20:19, Jonathan and David plan where they will meet next.

In similar fashion, in 1 Samuel 21:2, David misleads the priest Ahimelech into believing his army has been instructed to meet him at a certain location. Thus, it is likely the use of rally points was a common practice for David.

In 1 Samuel 30:9, David's army selects the Besor Valley as their rally point—where they rejoin the 200 exhausted soldiers in 1 Sam. 30:21. At times, rally points serve as convenient locations.

In 2 Samuel 15:27-28, David told his officials he would stay at a specific location to await messengers. He stated he would be in the fords of the wilderness—but he did not say exactly where. This was wise—considering the mass betrayals David was enduring at this time. In this plan, David did not state a specific location where he might be trapped.

In addition to planning rally points, you will need to plan for other contingencies. You will need a "bump" plan which will tell you where each individual warrior will go if his vehicle breaks down. You will need to plan for deaths—especially if your commanding officer dies. Who will be in charge of the mission then? You will also need plans for how to communicate in the case your radio breaks.

To properly frame your thinking, consider reading about Murphy's Law—which joking describes all the bad things which "could" and often do happen to military units. The unit which is best at adapting to problems often will be the one which is most successful on the battlefield. So, when you are training, constantly test your warriors on what they should do if certain scenarios take place. Warriors must be able to take problems in stride as they continue pressing forward with the mission.

Read Books

It has been noted: When one lacks experience, knowledge can serve as an adequate substitute. Of course, experience is preferred. But if a person lacks experience, reading books on a particular subject or culture can help.

For these reasons, if you are going to deploy to a certain region, it is prudent to read books which describe that country. Anything you can read will doubtlessly help you better relate to people in that region. Even fictional books written in that country may provide you with vast knowledge on regional customs, values and how individuals make decisions. All information is helpful. So, whenever you lack experience—read.

In the Bible, the warrior David studied history and used it to inform his decisions. . . .

In 2 Samuel 7:23, David reflects on the events of the Exodus—giving himself courage in the present. He explains how God defeated the Egyptian "gods." Therefore, David is confident in his own time that God is stronger than all other "gods" (2 Sam. 7:22).

Then, in 2 Samuel 11:18-21, Joab supposes David will lecture him on the history of the Judges in order to rebuke his poor leadership decision.

This means David had a reputation of using history to inform his perspective.

The answer is in books.
Read books.

Readiness

In 1 Samuel 23:1, we see David kept his army in a state of readiness. This allowed him to respond to emerging situations.

The U.S. Marines are a force in readiness—being prepared at all times to serve as America's 911 force. All military units should be prepared for war at all times.

If you are a military leader, you should constantly keep your troops in a physical and mental state of readiness. You never know when your unit will be called upon to serve in the midst of a crisis.

Your warriors should be mentally and physically prepared, properly trained and equipped to deploy at any time necessary. Use this concept of "readiness" to drive your leadership.

Train your warriors as if they will be required to perform their jobs in combat next week. Constantly ask yourself if you are confident your warriors could perform exceptionally and survive. Then, keep piling on training to push them hard to that standard. This is your best shot at helping your warriors to survive war. Train them hard so they can survive.

If you have this perspective, leadership will come natural to you. Frankly, if you train like you are going to war all the time, you will have a true sense of purpose as a leader. If you believe you are standing before men who will fight and die for our nation, you will be grave, temperate and measured, making the most of every teachable moment.

If you lead from this mindset, you will take issues seriously—recognizing that the same soldier who fails to follow an instruction to clean his weapon will be the same soldier who fails to follow vital instructions in war.

Leaders who lead from this perspective do everything they can to reform and train their personnel to a higher standard. It is this mindset which should compel you as a leader to be intrusive.

Take charge of your boys and make them battle-hardened warriors. Keep driving them and don't take your foot off the gas.

This is the proper mindset you need as a leader.

Reforming Troops

In 1 Samuel 22:2, it says 400 discontented, indebted or distressed men rallied to David to serve in his army. Thus, the army of David consisted of outcasts.

There is much to be said of David providing a place for outcasts.

Earlier as a boy, he chased down a lion and a bear to rescue a sheep (1 Sam. 17:34). Many shepherds would have given up on an attacked sheep. However, David does everything he can to rescue the damaged animals.

In similar fashion, David does not give up on society outcasts. Although others may have "given up" on these 400 men, David gives them a place in his company.

Later, this army of discontented warriors discusses stoning David after the destruction of their army base in Ziklag (1 Sam. 30:6-9). Rather than buckling under the pressure, David addresses the source of the grievance by immediately leading his army to fight the Amalekite raiders. Although David was confronted with the malcontent of his soldiers, he focused on leading, not bickering.

Finally, the restoration of David's outcasts occurs in 2 Samuel 2:3—when David is anointed king of Judah and brings his wilderness army with him into Hebron. Thus, the outcasts re-enter society with David.

While serving in the Marines, one of my favorite tasks involved reforming individuals which other leaders considered "troublemakers." It was an accomplishment indeed to see young men change— growing from troublemakers into proficient, dependable warriors who won competitions and were meritoriously promoted.

From David we learn the principle: Do not give up on your warriors. Reform outcasts. Keep them on your team as valued members.

How can you do this?

Level with a troublemaker one on one. Tell them your expectations—man to man. And tell them you are giving them a new chance to start with a fresh slate. Assign the person to another team with a different leader and different people. Then check back with them to make sure they are on the right track.

Don't give up on your people. Tell them your standard and keep applying pressure until they meet it.

Religion

Angel Army

In 2 Samuel 17:24, David makes Mahanaim the headquarters for his army during Absalom's rebellion. Interestingly, Mahanaim is the location where the patriarch, Jacob, saw a spectacular vision of angels—who were sent to protect him during his treacherous journey to meet with his brother, Esau (Gen. 32:1-2). In this way, the story of David somewhat mirrors the experience of Jacob. Whereas God showed Jacob the "glory" of angels sent to protect him; God sent a man, named Shobi, which means "glory" to provide David's army with bedding, bowls, pottery, wheat, barley, flour, grain, beans, honey, curds, sheep and cheese (2 Sam. 17:28-29).

Since David constantly saw God as a fortress of protection moving above him, it is possible his stay in Mahanaim also gave him visions of the angel camp which stood guard for him.

The ability to perceive God's activity around you can give you tremendous courage in the midst of danger (2 Kings 6:17). When our eyes are opened to the supernatural reality of God's protection around us we gain confidence to face whatever challenges lie before us.

True, depersonalization and derealization may be required for one to actually "see" these things. However, if you cannot actually "see" it, *choose* to see it within your mind of faith.

Faith is a choice. You can choose to see. And, by doing so, you will achieve the same tremendous courage.

Choose to see and you will see (2 Cor. 5:7).

Become a Spiritual Teacher

In 2 Samuel 5:10, it states God was with David. As a result he kept growing more and more powerful. Later within his Zion fortress, David shifted to his role as a religious leader for the Israelites. It is likely he penned many of his psalms during this time—reflecting on his past experiences. Thus, David's power was supernatural and spiritual. He grew in power as he led Israel further through his writing and teaching.

As you grow in your faith, look for opportunities to teach others. Help them to see what you see. Explain how you were able to overcome past obstacles by faith.

By teaching others you will grow stronger in your faith. Your teaching needs not be complicated. Simply share your story with others who would receive it humbly and benefit from it.

Called by God
God's calling can be revealed during prayer. . .
.

In 2 Samuel 2:1, David seeks and receives guidance from God in prayer. He is directed to move to Hebron, in Judah's territory, following the deaths of King Saul and Jonathan. Once there, he is anointed as the king of Judah (2 Sam. 2:4).

God's calling can also be revealed through others. . . .

In 2 Samuel 5:2, the leaders of Israel acknowledge the presence of the Lord abiding with David. In recognition of God's designation of David as His chosen leader, Israel asks David to serve as their king.

When one believes he is led by the Lord, he can gain confidence. If the person faces hardship he will be more determined to stay the course if he believes God called him to do so. This is the power contained within a calling from God. David's belief that God called him as the leader and king of his people gave him resolute determination.

Connection & Closeness with God
In 2 Samuel 6:12, David waits for the anger of God to subside before he resumes the movement of the ark. Earlier, the Lord was angry when the priest, Uzzah, irreverently touched the ark. David

essentially gives the Lord time for his anger to cool. When David witnesses blessing being poured out once again in the vicinity of the ark, David senses God's wrath has subsided.

Thus, David perception of the Lord is remarkably similar to Moses' perception. Moses saw God face-to-face (Exo. 33:11). Likewise David relates to the human emotions of God the Son.

How can a person develop the ability to perceive God? . . .

Spend time immersed in God's Word.

In order to know how God would feel about a certain thing, one must reflect on the character and works of God. Eventually as one spends significant time immersed in God's Word they begin to develop perception of God.

Kings were required to read from God's Word every day, thereby sharpening their ability to render justice based on God's commands (Deu. 17:19). In the Psalms it states priests recited verses aloud for the king (Psa. 45:1). Thus, the study of God's Word was a crucial component allowing David's close connection to the Lord.

And, when a person takes the time to know God, he develops the perception that God also knows him. . . .

In 2 Samuel 7:20, David said the Lord knows him. David perceived a connection with the Lord in his heart.

If you are looking to develop this closeness with God, read and listen to the Bible often. Then reflect carefully on how the passages are related to one another and how they apply to your life.

Divine Justice

In 2 Samuel 3:28-29, David asks God to judge Joab for his murder of Abner. In this case, David elects to look to God for help rather than ordering the execution of Judah's army general. David avoids making the hasty decision to execute Joab. Perhaps this was wise—considering Joab was a chief general and his execution may have caused a national crisis.

In the military we may be placed in impossible situations—where there are truly no good options. In some cases you may be compelled to act immediately to make what you determine to be the "best decision." However, in cases where you are not required to make a snap decision—don't.

Pause and let yourself think. Perhaps the situation will work itself out. You can even trust God to assist in this process.

For example, there were many situations I faced in the military where I was responsible for determining whether or not to award service-members non-judicial punishment (NJP). What I found was it was often best to see if situations would resolve themselves.

So, simply tell the offender to take a seat. Keep him nearby for a couple days and let him sweat as you slowly decide what to do. As the person sits, they imagine all the possible punishments they could get—and in doing so they at times convince themselves of their own guilt.

Sometimes a person can be best reformed when you do nothing—trusting God to transform them from the inside out.

Overall, remember all people are in the midst of their own journeys with God. Assist them on that path. Although you may be required to deliver punishment, do so only with the goal of promoting lasting life-long change in the individual. Your goal in delivering punishment is not to embarrass or crush, but to reform.

Thus, all your actions as a judge should mirror the actions of God—who desires that none should perish but for all to have everlasting life (Ezek. 18:23). When people mess up, use punishment to help them find the good path.

Relate to your soldiers as men who will one day be 80 years old. Use punishment to teach them the lessons they will need to carry them through the next 60 years of life. Don't give them a free pass because in the long run it will mean they will mess up again. Make the punishment memorable so they will later reflect back on their suffering, using it to dissuade themselves from making more bad decisions.

Endure Hardship to Gain God's Blessing

In 2 Samuel 16:5-13, David overlooks the cursing of a Benjamite who walked next to David's group as he fled Absalom's rebellion. Rather than assenting to Abishai, one of his warriors who wanted to kill the Benjamite, David chose to leave the Benjamite alone. David hopes the curses of the Benjamite will inspire God's increased blessing on himself.

This is not to say David had to earn God's favor. Rather, David thought if God desired to honor him, then anything which attempted to remove that honor would be confronted by God.

Later we see God reestablished David as king after the Absalom rebellion. And, by doing so, the curses of the Benjamite were rebuked by David's exaltation. In the end, David did not need to defend himself: God defended him.

Likewise, in all your travels you may feel tempted at times to act hastily, or to seek shortcuts. But, if you simply endure hardship and allow yourself to grow stronger through them, God will bless you in this process. At times all we can do is press forward.

Do not leave the good path set before you to chase fools. Nor should you depart on a fool's errand.

Endure.

Persevere. (Read Hebrews 11.)

Eternity

In 2 Samuel 12:23, David believes he will see his deceased son again in the afterlife.

For David, this thought is significant. David experienced many losses during his years as a warrior. Doubtlessly he coped with losses through his faith.

When we lose someone it is devastating. But if we believe physical death is not the end, it gives us something to look forward to—a light at the end of the tunnel.

Therefore, faith conquers death. Not even death itself is a barrier to the faithful. To the faithful, the "permanence" of death becomes "temporary"—a mere passage through which the individual continues living in the presence of God (Luke 20:38).

Thus, the concept of eternity is a powerful enhancement to a warrior. If the warrior removes fear—even fear of death, then they can gain an unshakable courage in the midst of incredible danger (1 Cor. 15:55). This is the power of faith.

When one follows the resurrected Lord Jesus—who Himself conquered over death and ascended into Heaven, there is no longer need for fear. Sure, some circumstances may cause a healthy fear to prompt us to protect ourselves. But, death itself is defeated by faith.

God with You

In 1 Samuel 16:18; 18:12, 14; 20:13 it says God was with David.

This imminent, felt presence of God next to the warrior gives him incredible courage. Thus, the warrior who moves with the Almighty becomes capable of achieving vastly more than they could relying on physical strength alone.

God is Superior to all other Supernatural Beings

In 1 Samuel 17:43, David completely dismisses the curses placed on him by Goliath. In this verse, Goliath curses David by his Philistine "gods."

In response we see although David is religious in his faith in the Lord God, he is altogether dismissive of other "gods." This means David was not superstitious in believing *anything*. In other words, if someone told David they put a voodoo hex on him, he would have dismissed it completely.

David wasn't scared of supernatural thoughts. Rather, his own supernatural thoughts dispelled all other supernatural thoughts. For David, his God was more powerful than any other spiritual being. Whereas Goliath talked about his "gods" from a distance; David was convinced his own God was on the battlefield with him (1 Sam. 17:47). With God within him and surrounding him, David had no need to fear the distant "gods" of Goliath. This imminent view of God was sufficient to imbue David with incredible courage and confidence for the battle.

In 2 Samuel 7:22, we see David believed his God to be completely unique and more powerful than any other "gods." This exclusivity in his religious beliefs would have granted David additional courage and confidence on the battlefield. Whereas other men may have thought it possible for the gods of others to defeat their own god; David altogether rejected this thought. In David's mind, there is no other supernatural being who is a match for his own God. Thus, David wielded an incredible spiritual enhancement to his battlefield abilities. He believed himself invincible through his direct association with God.

God's Plan

In 1 Samuel 24:6, David states his refusal to harm Saul because he is the "Lord's anointed" leader for the nation. Even though David was hunted by Saul, David refused to fight back. On at least two occasions, David could have killed Saul, but he chose to let him live (1 Sam. 24:11; 26:11).

David would have viewed Saul in the succession of the Judges. In the book of Judges, God would raise up judges for the specific purpose of helping the nation. Although the judges were imperfect, God wrought deliverance through them. Therefore, although Saul had imperfections, David refuses to harm him. To harm Saul would be to deprive Israel of the deliverance to be accomplished through him. Thus, David's reverence for the Lord keeps him from harming Saul.

In cases where we are not sure how our actions may affect the "big picture," it is good to have faith. Trust God is working to develop everything as a part of His good plan. Do not be hasty. Don't force yourself through an action which you may later regret.

Moreover, David's religion has a direct impact on his military strategy—informing him on specific actions (1 Sam. 22:5; 23:2-5; 2 Sam 2:1).

To keep himself accountable to God's plan, David travels with the priest Abiathar (1 Sam. 23:6).

In 2 Samuel 21:1, David seeks God's face to determine the cause of a three year famine.

In 2 Samuel 15:24-26, David brings the ark of the Lord with him as he flees during Absalom's rebellion. Thus, even in times of distress, David was drawn to worship as a source of strength.

In 2 Samuel 6:10, David diverts from his original plan to bring the ark to Jerusalem. After the death of the priest, Uzzah, as the result of an irreverent act, David opted for a compromise. He chose to bring the ark to the nearby settlement of Obed-Edom. This allowed David the needed time to research for the proper procedure for ark movement. Later, when David decided to resume movement of the ark, he was able to direct the priests to use the proper procedure—carrying it by poles (2 Sam. 6:13).

"Waiting on the Lord" helps us to remain encouraged in the midst of seemingly chaotic circumstances. Believe always that God will make sense out of the chaos you experience. Although God may not be causing the bad circumstances, He can use all bad things to your ultimate benefit in His good and perfect plan (Rom. 8:28).

This belief centers you. When other people become disheartened or confused, you will be capable of maintaining a level-head—thoroughly believing all things are controlled by God. This allows you to psychologically separate yourself from chaos as you focus on your own mission. This clarity is profound: Focus on your mission; trust God with the "big picture" of His plan.

Prayer

In 1 Samuel 23:2-4, David inquires of the Lord. God answers David—most likely through the mediation of the priest, Abiathar. Then, in 1 Samuel 23:10-12, David has a dialogue with the Lord in prayer.

This inner faith is the source of great courage and confidence. A person who believes God is directing his actions will become capable of greater feats. This faith in God is the source of David's battlefield ferocity.

Priestly Counsel

In 1 Samuel 28:17, the prophet Samuel declares David as the God-appointed successor to King Saul.

In 2 Samuel 12:7-12, the prophet Nathan declares God will allow judgment to come upon David in punishment for his offense against Uriah and Bathsheba. So, although God was with David in many situations for good, the presence of the Lord upon David also brought God's accountability upon him when he sinned.

In 2 Samuel 21:1, David prayed to seek God's counsel concerning a three year famine. God heard his prayer and granted him an answer—most likely through David's priest or prophet.

No matter where your travels take you, always seek out a good spiritual relationship with another to help you to remain centered. Another spiritual warrior who is serving with you may provide you much needed accountability and encouragement during hardships you may encounter.

Sacrifice & Offerings

In 2 Samuel 24:22-24, David refuses to offer sacrifices to the Lord for which he did not pay. Thus, David's offerings were sacrificial and cost him personally.

In 2 Samuel 6:13, 17-18, David participates in sacrifices to the Lord. David wears a linen ephod—which was likely very similar to the garments of priests during the sacrifices.

Be a giving person, who is charitable—ever looking for opportunities to change the world around you for good. Entire communities can be transformed by sincere people who simply do their part to help others.

Sacred Objects

In 1 Samuel 23:9, David uses the ephod in his prayers to determine his next step in a crisis. As he travels he brings with him both the priest Abiathar and the sacred ephod. Later, David brought the ark into Jerusalem so it could be near his royal palace (2 Sam. 6:12). Then, when David flees from the capital during Absalom's rebellion, he takes the ark with him (2 Sam. 15:24-26). This shows David found confidence within sacred objects.

Although an object itself might not contain inherent supernatural power, at times they may give us additional courage and confidence. Anything a warrior can do to increase his courage can be greatly beneficial. So, if you can gain additional courage by wearing a cross necklace, or an extra "dog tag" with a Bible verse, do so.

This is what I did. During multiple combat deployments I had a "dog tag" with Joshua 1:9—constantly reminding me to remain strong and courageous because God was with me wherever I went.

Often the toughest battles are fought within our minds as we muster the courage to act. Perhaps a sacred object could give you the additional edge you need as a warrior.

Supernatural Vision = Power & Confidence

In 2 Samuel 5:10, it states God was with David. As a result he kept growing more and more powerful.

So, how did David develop this supernatural power?

On a basic level, David served in practical religious activities which helped him to grow his faith. David wrote Psalms and taught others.

On a more advanced level, David was filled with the Holy Spirit (Psa. 51:11).

As David penned many psalms, he thoroughly reflected on his past experiences. Therefore, David's supernatural power grew as he wrestled with his faith through his past experiences.

In other words, the Psalms show David learned to see God in all his past experiences. This resulted in an incredibly powerful faith—which gave David surges of courage and confidence.

David's faith grew so much he actually began to "see" God as an immense supernatural fortress who travelled above him at all times. This is why David often referred to God as his refuge, fortress and stronghold throughout the Psalms (Psa. 2:12; 5:11; 7:1; 8:2; 9:9; 11:1; 14:6; 16:1; 17:7; 18:2, 30-31, 46; 19:14; 25:20; 27:1, 5; 28:1, 8; 31:1-4, 19-20; 34:8, 22; 36:7; 37:39-40; 40:2; 52:7; 55:8; 57:1; 59:1, 9, 16-17; 61:2-4; 62:2, 6-8; 64:10; 95:1; 141:8; 142:4-5; 144:1-2).

As David walked onto battlefields, he viewed God's presence as a great spiritual castle overshadowing his entire army—protecting him from Heaven. This is not figurative or mere poetry: David actually experienced visions of God.

To capture a picture of what this fortress looked like to David, a similar vision might be found in Ezekiel 1—where the glory of God appeared like an immense castle machine to the prophet Ezekiel.

Also, it is no coincidence David's battle headquarters during the Absalom rebellion was located at Mahanaim—meaning "two camps." At this location God's supernatural activity was revealed previously (Gen. 32:1-2). Wherever David moved, he saw the Lord moving within a supernatural camp above his own army camp.

This thought is profound—and it doubtlessly helped David during all his battles. If one's faith can progress to the point that he can "see" God as a divine fortress moving with him, then his battlefield actions will be imbued with supernatural power. Physically, David was a powerful, proficient warrior. However, spiritually, David was unstoppable—being capable of fighting to physical exhaustion, then beyond. Thus, David's supernatural visions of God helped him to fight better than his foes.

So, how did David develop such strong faith?

In my book, <u>Dear David: Learning to See God through PTSD, Anxiety and Depression</u>, I explain the profound, remarkably beneficial effects of David's post-traumatic stress disorder (PTSD) upon his worldview. Indeed, the PTSD symptoms of depersonalization and derealization would have provided a natural means through which God strengthened David. These PTSD symptoms assisted David in his ability to visualize God's activity around him and within him.

Travelling with God

In 2 Samuel 7:2-3, the prophet Nathan declares God is with David. Later, God declares to David He has been with him throughout all his travels (2 Sam. 7:9).

Although we may "feel" alone, the fact is God never abandons us (Josh. 1:9). No matter where we may find ourselves, we can be confident God is sticking with us through whatever we face.

Our hardships may be great. But, we know for sure God's presence lessens them so we have the strength to bear them. So, the promise of God's presence "with us" is a powerful encouragement. Things may be tough. But with God's presence abiding with us we find a way to endure through all things—culminating in the receiving of the crown of eternal life which will be granted to all the faithful (Rom. 8:28; Rev. 2:10).

May the peace of God rest upon you— wherever you may be found.

<u>Repentance & Paying Amends</u>

In 2 Samuel 12:13, David immediately repented of his sin against Uriah when he was confronted by Nathan the prophet. Although there is no way for David to pay amends due to Uriah being dead, one could say David still attempted to pay retribution by doing right by Bathsheba. Later, one of Bathsheba's sons—Solomon, was named heir to David's throne. Solomon was named heir even though he was not the firstborn son of David—which may be the result of David paying fourfold for his sin (2 Sam. 12:6).

In 2 Samuel 21:2-7, David hears the grievance of the Gibeonites against Saul. Although a most bizarre resolution was reached from our perspective, David allowed ancient justice to be achieved.

In 2 Samuel 24:10, David is conscience-stricken after taking the census of Israel. He prays and asks God for forgiveness.

If you have done something wrong, own up to it. Have the moral courage to admit to your wrongs—especially if you should have done better for your subordinates. Everyone can respect "we are all human, and we all make mistakes." Do not shy away from saying you made a misstep. Own it, and take action to repair the wrong done. Know yourself and seek self-improvement.

Reserves

In 1 Samuel 30:9, David allows 200 soldiers to rest while his other 400 soldiers fight the Amalekites. This serves a good purpose. Those who remain behind guarded the supplies of those who continued the pursuit (1 Sam. 30:24). So, although they were too exhausted to continue, they helped the other soldiers by lightening their load. The soldiers who pressed forward did not have to keep carrying their full load of equipment. They left all the non-essential stuff with the remain-behind element of the unit.

The concept of "reserves" is often misunderstood—with people wrongly conflating this concept with part-time soldiers. But, all units have a "reserve" built into them for each mission. It is essential. This is how it works . . .

If you are assigned as a mission leader, do this for the best success . . .

Take the total number of your troops and divide them into three groups. Your first group will be a direct assault element. Your second group will be a flanking element. And your third group will be the reserve.

Understood so far?

The first group lays down cover fire. The second group maneuvers to the flank of your enemy. You hold the third "reserve" group out of the fight. At the decisive moment, you signal instructions to your reserve. This allows you to immediately reinforce whatever action which will have the best effect.

In other words, your "reserve" is always the "Ace" up your sleeve. You do not play an Ace until it is the exact moment when it helps you to win big.

This is the true purpose of a reserve. And, remarkably this concept of dividing a unit in thirds is found throughout the Bible.

In 2 Samuel 12:29, after Joab and the army cut off the water supply in the siege of Rabbah, David gathers the remaining forces/people to make a final rush on the city. In other words, David finally commits the reserve troops to the battle, using their fresh strength to push within the city.

If ever you are tasked with a mission—always remember this principle: (1) Divide your force into three groups, (2) Make one group "direct assault," another group "flank assault," and the third group "reserve." (3) Engage the enemy with this simple pattern.

When considering who to put in each group, put the fastest people in the "flank assault" group, and the best shooters in the "direct assault" group.

If you must do continuous operations, trade fighters from the first groups into the "reserve" group as necessary to give them a relative break. For example, if some of your fastest warriors from the "flank assault" group are tired, allow them to get some relative rest in the "reserve" group while a fresh "reserve" warrior fills his spot in the "flank assault" group. This allows you to keep all your horses healthy.

The above is a very simple, memorable structure which can help you in warfare, so commit it to your memory. It provides a good structure to help you to organize any unit very rapidly if you are ever tasked with a mission with a short amount of time to prepare.

For example, let's say someone told me now to take charge of 100 soldiers. This is what I would say . . .

"All machine gunners and rifle experts line up here. (Point)"

"All my best runners line up here. (Point)"

With these two commands I would immediately make the structure for each of the groups. The machine gunners and rifle experts are in the "direct assault" and the best runners are in the "flank assault." Others are in the "reserve."

From here I would simply sift through the individuals. For example, two machine gunners might be fast runners, so I might choose to put them in the flank group rather than direct assault. Then I would assign a leader for each of the three groups.

As we move to the battlefield, I would place myself in whatever group I determined there would be the most friction—or largest chance something might go wrong. So my job would be to provide corrective instructions as we fire and maneuver.

Please remember this because it might save your life and the lives of your people in a pinch.

<u>Siege</u>

Sieges are effective because they put the defending army in a desperate position where they have only two options: (1) hide within the city, remaining until starvation; or (2) make a desperate attack on the surrounding force.

In 2 Samuel 11:23-24 we see siege warfare was used as an effective means of seizing a city. The siege culminates when Joab exhausts the city's water supply (2 Sam. 12:27). Then David leads a final attack to move within the city (2 Sam. 12:29).

Earlier David also used siege warfare to seize Jerusalem from the Jebusites. The Jebusites attempted to remain within the city—boasting their city was impenetrable. However David leads his army to break into the city via the water shafts—bringing a stunning end to the siege.

Although it is not likely you will need to perform a siege, you can learn much from this ancient method of warfare. Siege warfare was a good option for ancient armies because it prevented open battle and high losses of life.

So, in your military planning, consider how you can accomplish your mission to minimize loss of life. Exploit your enemy's vulnerabilities, rather than facing him in open battle.

For example, if you determine the location of your enemy's resupply route, and you destroy a bridge on this route, this will prevent his resupply. And by denying your enemy fuel and supplies you can bring him to his culminating point rapidly—compelling surrender.

The ideal victory is the one in which you suffer zero casualties and defeat your enemy before he can react. Be creative. Think about what your enemy needs most, then find creative ways to deny him. This is how the most effective military leaders plan.

Effective military leaders work to win battles before they enter the battlefield. Reflect on this.

Simplicity & Homesickness

Simplicity

As a warrior, it is good to discipline yourself. Know yourself and be yourself. Become comfortable in your gear and at home in your surroundings. Find contentment. Within this inner simplicity you can find peace anywhere you roam.

In the Bible, the skilled warrior David exemplifies this simplicity and contentment. . . .

In 1 Samuel 16:11, David appears handsome as he comes in from the fields. A similar description is found in 1 Samuel 16:18 and 17:42.

In 1 Samuel 17:38-39, David refuses to wear the standard issue armor common for other soldiers.

In 1 Samuel 18:4, David's military gear is simple, including a robe, belt, sword and bow.

In 1 Samuel 18:18, when David was offered the daughter of King Saul, he refused on the objection that he was a common man unworthy of royalty.

In 2 Samuel 5:12, it says David "knew" the Lord made him king for the sake of the people of Israel. Thus, David did not take credit for the successes of his kingship. Nor did David claim he was appointed for his own good. David considered himself as a mere servant of God and His people.

In 2 Samuel 6:20-22, David revels in the pleasures of simple worship—desiring above all to please God, even if it draws the criticism of others.

In 2 Samuel 7:8, the Lord says through the prophet Nathan that David was taken from among the sheep flock and raised up to serve Israel as king. Thus, David had a humble beginning, which became a noteworthy part of his character as king. In his heart, David ever desired to care for his people the same way he cared for his sheep.

David was a common, humble, young shepherd who demonstrated how the power of God can work through a simple person. For the common people, David was inspiring because he represented what they desired to become—simple people filled with God's power.

So, within the songs of 1 Samuel 18:6-7, we foreshadow the vast impact David will have on Bible spirituality. David's simplicity made his example attainable to the common people. Therefore, he gained popularity within Judah and Israel (1 Sam. 18:16).

Homesickness

When others feel inclined toward homesickness, and their sentiment slowly draws their hearts to sadness; you choose to dig your spiritual roots into the land on which you stand.

Recognize you are where you are for a purpose, and God is walking with you through it all (Joshua 1:5-9). Find enjoyment within yourself and allow that peace to settle over you—even if you are in the midst of chaos. God will be with you no matter what (Isa. 41:10; Heb. 13:5).

Although David longed to return to his home inheritance, he found peace in the invisible stronghold of the Lord—which moved above and with him during all his travels (Psa. 2:12; 5:11; 7:1; 8:2; 9:9; 11:1; 14:6; 16:1; 17:7; 18:2, 30-31, 46; 19:14; 25:20; 27:1, 5; 28:1, 8; 31:1-4, 19-20; 34:8, 22; 36:7; 37:39-40; 40:2; 52:7; 55:8; 57:1; 59:1, 9, 16-17; 61:2-4; 62:2, 6-8; 64:10; 95:1; 141:8; 142:4-5; 144:1-2).

Likewise, may you find peace wherever you travel—realizing God is moving incredible spiritual machines above you, caring for you in unseen ways during all your journeys. An angel army will attend to you, giving you peace which passes all understanding.

And, in God's presence you are always home. By holding to this thought you will find inner peace wherever you roam.

Situational Awareness, Scouts & Informants

Situational Awareness

"Situational awareness" is gained and maintained as a warrior understands factors at play around him. At all times, gather information. It may seem as if some information may be irrelevant, but a smart warrior will choose to incorporate all information into his plan.

Although you might not be able to attend all meetings, or be present in all situations, make it a habit to employ your subordinates to gather information for you. Then have planning sessions with your team, where you discuss the best opportunities presented within situations—taking advantage of concurrent events and occurrences. This allows you to exploit all situations to your benefit.

In 1 Samuel 20:5, David puts in a "request for information" with his battle buddy, Jonathan. While Jonathan gathers more information for him, David hides in a field. This allows David to make decisions based on better "situational awareness," rather than making decisions based on partial information.

Be wise and pray for wisdom. Knowledge is power. An enemy can be decisively brought to his culminating point if you exploit known vulnerabilities. So, in all cases, always gather information about everything. Discuss it with your

---

fellow leaders. Think creatively and find ways to exploit everything to your advantage.

You should even use the weather to your advantage. Everything is relevant, and if you plan well you can orchestrate everything into a seamless plan which is capable of matching multiple contingency scenarios.

Scouts, Infiltrators & Spies

Scouts allow a military commander to gain situational awareness while keeping his main force in a relatively safe position.

In 1 Samuel 26:4, David sends scouts to determine Saul's location. In this case, David's scouts gather offensive information—allowing David to determine the exact location of Saul's camp.

In 1 Samuel 30:16, rather than deploying scouts, David chooses to scout the Amalekite army location himself. Considering the recent mutinous comments of his soldiers in 1 Samuel 30:6, it was indeed a good decision to avoid relying on his soldiers for this vital scouting mission.

Scouts can also be used as infiltrators. Although David could have fought and crushed Absalom's rebellion, he avoided direct confrontation. Instead, David prayed for God to bring peaceful resolution through bad counselors (2 Sam. 15:31). God immediately answers David's prayer by sending

Hushai—whom David sends to infiltrate Absalom's council.

Then, in 2 Samuel 15:27-28, David establishes spies within Absalom's rebellion by sending Abiathar and Zadok as infiltrators. David instructs Hushai to pass information to them as his messengers (2 Sam. 15:32-36). Due to their designation as priests, Abiathar and Zadok were good choices for messengers—allowing them to bypass normal restrictions due to their ecclesiastical responsibilities. Whereas a common man travelling to David's camp might have been suspected of treason; priests could state they were travelling for the purpose of providing religious services to those within David's camp. The plan was successful in 2 Sam. 17:15-22.

Smart huh?

Using priests as spies was a good idea—because they would have been under less suspicion.

However, in this example, there is also a warning: You must be wary of *everyone*.

Anyone could be a spy.

Informants
In 1 Samuel 30:11-16, David captures a man who he suspects was involved in the raiding of his military base in Ziklag. David treats the exhausted Egyptian with compassion, providing him with food and water. David's humane treatment transformed

this man into an informant. David's decision to feed the prisoner allows him to obtain vital information—leading David to the Amalekite army camp.

In war, the humane treatment of prisoners can be used to obtain helpful information. However, be wary at first. Any prisoner of war with a weapon should have ammunition for his weapon at the time of his capture. If a prisoner of war <u>does not have ammunition</u>, this means he only surrendered after he made every effort to kill you. However, if a prisoner of war <u>has ammunition</u>, this means he may have a higher likelihood of being sympathetic and serving as your informant.

Stealth & Concealment

Concealment & Hiding

When outnumbered or unsure of your surroundings, it is wise to remain concealed. Often when waiting to gather more information it is good to hold off movement.

In 1 Samuel 20:5, 24, David hides while waiting for more information to be gathered by Jonathan.

When in doubt, remain concealed and send scouts to gather more information. If you sense your location may be compromised, quickly move to a different place.

Stealth

Stealth enables a warrior to quickly and quietly close distances to his enemy.

In 1 Samuel 24:4, David sneaks up to Saul in a cave, cutting off a corner of his robe.

Then, in 1 Samuel 26:7-8, David and Abishai sneak into Saul's camp while his entire army is asleep.

In these cases, David's stealth gave him a decisive advantage over Saul. However, David does not take credit for his stealthy ability—rather declaring the Lord as the source of this skill (1 Sam. 26:12). This is significant.

So how did David master the ability to use stealth?

Of course, David's physical prowess as a warrior was a part of his stealth ability. Elsewhere in the Bible it explains David was a dancer, who actually had the ability to dodge spears thrown at him. So, David was very slippery, and it is likely he would rapidly glide away from enemy strikes when engaged in hand-to-hand combat.

But, beyond this, David's PTSD further enhanced his stealth ability. David's general hypervigilance and social impairment would have lent him an abiding wariness of others. This is seen throughout the Psalms—where David constantly suspected people of plotting against him. This means David would have always guessed the motives and actions of people and planned accordingly—allowing him to anticipate their movements and meet them at future points.

In other words, his astute, hypervigilant predictions of the actions of others allowed him to lead them—going to the point where they "would" be moments later. Therefore, David's attacks on others may have been akin to "ambushes"—where he would constantly guess his opponent's next move and intercept them at those points. This would explain how David achieved the ability to dodge spears.

Moreover, David's PTSD gave him a sense of depersonalization—where he felt somewhat separated from himself. This is difficult to explain, but depersonalization would have granted David an increased sense of his own agility.

This would explain why David often credited God for his own military successes. As David moved, his consciousness would toggle in and out in its perception of his body's position. So, if David were running forward, depersonalization would have made it seem to David as if he were running, but during the gaps of conscious perception that the Lord was running *through* him. In other words, David interpreted the depersonalization gaps as moments where the Lord essentially took over his body and moved it for him.

Therefore, when understanding David's PTSD we are able to see David *actually* viewed his physical actions as the actions of God Himself. Thus, David's praise for God's acts are not merely poetic as they might be interpreted by those who do not understand PTSD. Rather, David's actions truly were the actions of God as he moved David's body during depersonalization gaps.

In other words, God worked through the PTSD disability of David to bring about His will— just as God continues to work through our own unique situations. David was in many ways broken by his PTSD, but God turned this "disability" into a blessing on the battlefield and beyond.

This concept extends much further however. Throughout David's psalms there are many times in which he describes events as though he is experiencing them from within the Lord Jesus' body. This is also an effect of PTSD depersonalization—where God used this common PTSD symptom to communicate messianic prophecy to David. Then, following David, future prophets borrowed his method of depersonalization prophecy—describing future events as they were experienced by the Lord Jesus and those near him.

This is a very interesting concept. If you would like to learn more about this topic, read my book, <u>Dear David: Learning to See God through PTSD, Anxiety and Depression</u>.

Overall, combat PTSD is means of developing many warrior skills, in addition to serving as the pathway to understanding Bible prophecy.

Unit Stealth Ability

Being stealthy and training your unit to be stealthy, translates to an ability to quickly move—gliding around an enemy while remaining undetected. In 2 Samuel 5:23, David uses a circling maneuver to position his army to attack the Philistines. This demonstrates David's ability to quickly move troops in a stealthy manner.

So, if you are good at hiding, and you train all your people to be good at it, then your entire unit will be more capable of executing flanking attacks. As a flanking unit, be swift, silent and deadly.

<u>Subordinate Leaders</u>

Remember our discussion of "threes," and how as a matter of principle military units should be divided into multiple parts. No matter what you are in charge of, always apply this model to your unit—understanding the "three" format gives you the ability to rotate warriors in and out of battle into the reserve group. This principle is strikingly important and is visible in military units all the way to the highest levels of command. And it is founded by warriors like David in the Bible.

By dividing units into three parts it means you must appoint leaders to be in charge of each group. Throughout David's lifetime we see David used this basic division of units to grant significant authority to his subordinate leaders. . . .

In 2 Samuel 18:1 during Absalom's rebellion, David appointed army "commanders over thousands" and "commanders over hundreds." Then David sends out the army under the command of three generals—Joab, Abishai, and Ittai (2 Sam. 18:2).

In 2 Samuel 2:13-32, Joab is the general who leads David's army in a civil war between Judah and Israel. Joab is one of three brothers. One of Joab's brothers, Abishai, was with David while he was fleeing from Saul (1 Sam. 26:6). However, Joab and Asahel do not emerge within David's army until he is anointed king of Judah. It could be that Joab was one of the discontented, indebted men within David's wilderness army. Or it could be that Joab emerged as a leader from within Judah's population after a recommendation from Abishai. Either way, Joab quickly obtains general status in David's army.

Joab later leads Judah's forces on a raid (2 Sam. 3:22).

In 2 Samuel 10:7-13, Joab and Abishai lead Israel's army in battle against the Arameans and Ammonites.

In 2 Samuel 11:1, David trusts Joab to lead Israel's army. This is different from King Saul—who it appears was intent upon leading all expeditions personally. Thus, trusting in subordinate leaders allows a leader more flexibility—and in this case it allowed David to rest from warfare.

So, whenever you establish divisions within your unit, ensure you appoint good leaders over each group. Inform them of your intent. Then trust those leaders to carry out your instructions.

Last, in leadership always "inspect what you expect."

Never forget that. Do not blindly trust your subordinates. Inspect them often. Have them brief you on all aspects of their operations and decisions. And over time they will *earn* your trust.

Give them slack with lesser issues to test how they will react and how they will choose to brief you. And in doing this you will find the delicate balance which must be maintained by you as the leader.

Remember, you can delegate "authority" to your subordinate leaders, but you cannot delegate "responsibility." Ultimately you are responsible for everything your subordinate leaders do, so make sure they are doing things properly.

Inspect what you expect.

<u>Supernatural Power</u>

In 1 Samuel 16:13 it says the Holy Spirit gave David power. In my book, <u>Dear David: Learning to See God through PTSD, Anxiety and Depression</u>, I attribute this spiritual power to David's PTSD derealization. David constantly viewed God as a supernatural fortress/refuge/stronghold which moved with and above him—providing him an endless supply of strength in the midst of all hardships (Psa. 2:12; 5:11; 7:1; 8:2; 9:9; 11:1; 14:6; 16:1; 17:7; 18:2, 30-31, 46; 19:14; 25:20; 27:1, 5; 28:1, 8; 31:1-4, 19-20; 34:8, 22; 36:7; 37:39-40; 40:2; 52:7; 55:8; 57:1; 59:1, 9, 16-17; 61:2-4; 62:2, 6-8; 64:10; 95:1; 141:8; 142:4-5; 144:1-2). Perhaps this spiritual vision was similar to the vision of Ezekiel 1.

So, although your traumatic experiences may affect you deeply, they provide a pathway to a deeper connection with God. As you develop as a warrior, be mindful of the spiritual path. Faith is a powerful enhancement to a warrior—granting supernatural courage and resolve.

Take the pathway of David. Gain power from the spiritual world around you. God offers it freely in Christ (Rev. 22:17).

Supplies & Resources

Know what resources are available and how to get them. Stockpile things your troops need.

Know the specializations of other adjacent units and form relationships with your peers in those units. Perhaps they can offer something to help your unit, and vice versa.

In the Bible, we see the warrior David procured resources from people adjacent to him . . .

In 2 Samuel 5:11, David receives resources and skilled workers from Hiram, king of Tyre, to build his Jerusalem palace. These include cedar logs, stonemasons and carpenters.

In 2 Samuel 12:31, David placed garrisons within Ammonite territory after capturing the city, Rabbah. In these garrisons, David's army supervised labor within Ammonite settlements—commanding them to make bricks.

In 2 Samuel 16:1, Ziba provides bread, raisins, figs and wine to David's people as they fled from Absalom's rebellion. Although Ziba was using this gift in an attempt to deceive David, ultimately David saw through his trickery (2 Sam. 16:3-4). In the meantime, however, David's party enjoyed the food provisions in the wilderness.

In 2 Samuel 17:24, David makes Mahanaim the headquarters for his army during Absalom's rebellion. Interestingly, Mahanaim is the location where the patriarch, Jacob, saw a spectacular vision of angels—who were sent to protect him during his treacherous journey to meet with his brother, Esau (Gen. 32:1-2). In this way, the story of David somewhat mirrors the experience of Jacob. Whereas God showed Jacob the "glory" of angels sent to protect him; God sent a man, named Shobi, which means "glory" to provide David's army with bedding, bowls, pottery, wheat, barley, flour, grain, beans, honey, curds, sheep and cheese (2 Sam. 17:28-29).

In 2 Samuel 19:32 it says a man, named Barzillai, provided for David's army while they were camped in Mahanaim during Absalom's rebellion.

Always think ahead. . . .

If your supply lines were severed, where would your unit get water, ammunition and food?

If your normal re-fueling method is compromised, what is an alternate means of obtaining fuel?

Do you have enough supplies to hold off an attacking force?

If *Plan A* is a no-go, what is your *Plan B* and *Plan C*?

During your deployment, constantly revisit this thought to ensure you are not caught unprepared and stranded from help. Squirrel away resources. Don't get knocked out of the fight on a technicality. Don't allow your enemy to culminate you over something as silly as water, ammo or food. Have bump plans for everything—including your essential supplies.

If in any case you find yourself cut off, or perceive your enemy is moving to cut you off from your supplies, it is vital you move quickly to reestablish that connection. Supplies are your lifeblood. You cannot survive long-term without them.

Move closer to the area from which your supplies will be arriving. Use your radios to establish air contact. Do whatever you can to quickly regain your connection with your lifeblood.

Tact, Humility & Professionalism

Warriors may be socially impaired or otherwise limited in their abilities to relate to others in social settings. For warriors who have been exposed to the terrors of battle, PTSD may result in them developing increased social impairment as a result of certain PTSD symptoms—such as hypervigilance.

So, how can a warrior with PTSD continue to operate in social settings?

By using tact.

Typically if someone is kind and formal with others, they will be likeable.

Throughout the lifetime of David, we see he would often counteract his social impairment (which is evidenced in his psalms) by simply focusing upon being properly tactful in social situations . . .

In 1 Samuel 18:18, when David was offered the daughter of King Saul, he refused on the objection that he is a common man unworthy of royalty. In my first book, <u>Dear David: Learning to See God through PTSD, Anxiety and Depression</u>, I explain the PTSD "social impairment" of David. For David, he was not merely being humble. Rather, he was expressing his deeply seated belief that he was unworthy as a part of his social impairment.

Nevertheless, his humble reply is what made David increasingly more likeable.

In 1 Samuel 20:5-6, even after fleeing from King Saul, David continues professional appearances by sending a message to the king via Jonathan. This tactful action ensured David would receive a proper excuse in the case he had a misunderstanding. Remarkably, even in the midst of danger, David takes measures to maintain his professional responsibilities.

In 1 Samuel 22:3, David asks permission from the king of Moab to allow his parents to stay within the stronghold.

In 1 Samuel 24:8-16, David speaks to King Saul with tact—even when David's life was threatened. In this discussion, David refers to Saul as "king," "lord," and anointed. David also bows before him in reverence. A similar situation is found in 1 Samuel 26:17-20.

In 1 Samuel 27:5, David refers to himself as the "servant" of King Achish. David entreats Achish for an assigned city where his army can camp. During his time in Philistine territory, David kept up tactful appearances with King Achish as a part of his deception (see 1 Sam. 27:7-11).

In 1 Samuel 30:18, David's army plunders the Amalekite raiders—taking livestock and their families who were kidnapped from Ziklag. David uses some of the extra plunder to send gifts to the elders of Judah (1 Sam. 30:26-31). Three days after David's return to Ziklag, he learns of the deaths of Saul and Jonathan (2 Sam. 1:1-2). So, the plunder gifts sent to the elders of Judah served a purpose in his imminent appointment as the king of Judah (2 Sam. 2:4).

In 2 Samuel 7:27-29, David refers to himself as the servant of the Lord. Although at many times David is raw with the Lord in his psalms, David's default position was to demonstrate tact when interacting with the Lord through his prophet or priest.

In serious settings, such as funerals, David also uses tact to counteract his severe inward emotions. . . .

In 2 Samuel 1:17-27, David shows great tact in his mourning lament composed for Saul and Jonathan. In this lament, David makes no mention of Saul's mistakes, nor his mistreatments of David. Rather, David focuses only on positive aspects of Saul and his kingship. This is indeed graceful of David—to be wronged by Saul, yet still granting him dignity in the end.

In 2 Samuel 3:31-39, David mourns and grieves at the funeral of Abner. He states he is so saddened by the events that he does not have the strength to preside in judgment over Joab for the murder (2 Sam. 3:39). Instead, David asks the Lord to judge Joab.

At times, David's PTSD impairments made him emotionally crippled. In this way, this above event where he fails to judge Joab is similar to his emotional inability to judge Absalom (2 Sam. 13:33), and an earlier account where he failed to punish the rapist of Tamar (2 Sam. 13:21). David was a man broken by combat in many ways—which was apparent in his social impairment.

Rather than venting his emotions in public, David found a more favorable outlet in his prayers and the writing of his psalms. This is the ultimate form of humility—anonymity. David looks inward in the development of his own spirituality—taking inventory of his candid thoughts and emotions, and later choosing to share these psalms with others. Whereas David's psalms contain his passionate, unfiltered emotions; David's social interactions with people typically reflect his intentional effort to mask his feelings with tactfulness.

So, if you ever find yourself struggling to remain composed in social settings, revert to good mannered tactfulness and humility. Using tact will allow you to get through social situations until you can seclude yourself within your own prayers and reflections—similar to the successful method used by the warrior David.

Be professional. Be kind. Then later unwind.

<u>Teamwork & Allies</u>

What is an ally?

An ally is a person or group who assists you in your mission.

No matter where you find yourself within the military, it is important to start making friends . . . and to have as many friends as possible. The person you help today may be the person who helps you tomorrow.

Consider boot camp . . .

Simply put, boot camp is designed to get you out of your comfort zone. No one is good at everything. Eventually even the strongest person needs help with something. So, boot camp is designed to bring those personal weaknesses to the surface to get individuals to look to one another for strength. Shared adversity is the path to becoming a team.

At the beginning of boot camp, no one really cares when drill instructors weed out non-hackers.

But, as boot camp progresses there should be a shift in how recruits think. The old patterns of thinking as an individual should be replaced by "team-thinking."

The recruits should make sure their fellows all graduate with them. When others are hurt you carry them—refusing to leave behind your buddy.

Thus, drill instructors instill this "teamwork" amongst recruits by playing a specific role. The drill instructor plays the part of the adversary, compelling recruits to band together and work as a team.

Then, this simple "team" mentality should carry with the person throughout his entire time in the military. As a leader you should have solid peer-to-peer contacts in every other unit around you. This makes it so you can call in favors in a pinch.

Likewise, your subordinate leaders should do the same within their own peer groups. This approach will offer you several possible avenues to obtain help in difficult times. For example, if your contact falls through, perhaps you can rely on one of your subordinate leaders' contacts.

During deployments this is how things are often accomplished. Establishing and maintaining these contacts could be the only way for you to get gear or other supplies or receive support.

During my deployments I made friends with everyone because you never know what will happen. I even made friends with the Corpsmen at the Shock-Trauma medical tent on one of the bases.

Why?

I reasoned within myself if they knew me *personally,* and if I or my people were injured, this personal connection may push them further to do their uttermost to save us.

So, I had the guys on my team teach all the Corpsmen how to shoot all my different machineguns. They thought it was great getting to learn and in return I got the peace of mind knowing perhaps these skilled professionals would go the extra mile to help us if ever we found ourselves in need.

Also by requiring my team members to teach Corpsmen how to fire it made my team even more proficient in weapons. In this way, my friendship with this adjacent unit was very positive—providing necessary training to those who lacked it, making my team more proficient with weapons, and giving me peace of mind knowing my buddies would be looking out for me if harm visited us.

Likewise, you need to make buddies everywhere.

Allies provide supplies . . .

Allies can provide things for you which you cannot get for yourself. Often in the military an unofficial trade system exists—where people help one another to the mutual benefit of both people. In some cases this allows the individual to bypass normal time requirements, or to get extra help.

Of course, the individual could just wait, but in cases where you are pressed for time, it helps to have allies everywhere so you can get help as soon as possible. It is during times where we are desperate we need allies the most. So, when you are not desperate it makes sense to help others and to build those friendships which may be necessary for your later success.

Very early in David's military life, he went to the priest, Ahimelech, when he was fleeing from King Saul. In the Lord's house, David asked for a sword and food (1 Sam. 21:1-8).

Later, when David's son, Absalom, rebelled against David and chased him from Jerusalem, David's military was offered food and supplies by people they met in the wilderness. In 2 Samuel 16:1, Ziba provides bread, raisins, figs and wine to David's people as they fled from Absalom's rebellion. In return, David later ensures Ziba receives a land allotment (2 Sam. 19:29).

Then, in 2 Samuel 19:32 it says a man, named Barzillai, provided for David's army while they were camped in Mahanaim during Absalom's rebellion. In return for his kindness, David offered to bring Barzillai to Jerusalem with him. Although Barzillai could not go with David, he sent his servant Kimham in his stead (2 Sam. 19:37).

In another situation, after David defeats some Arameans in battle, he gains an ally (2 Sam. 8:9-10): Tou, king of Hamath, congratulates David and sends him gifts of gold, silver and bronze. Previously Tou was at war with Hadadezer, so David's defeat of his forces benefited Tou.

Allies provide skills . . .

In some cases we frankly do not have the skills we need to accomplish a certain mission. So, stay in tune with what allies could possibly do for you. When talking to your friends, tell them what you can do to help them. Ask them questions about what they do. Think creatively. Try to figure out how they might be able to help you in a pinch.

For example, when David was fleeing from Absalom in 2 Samuel 15:30-31, he prayed for God to frustrate the advisors of his betrayer. Immediately, in answer to his prayer, one of David's friends, named Hushai, arrived. David immediately asks Hushai to infiltrate Absalom's council to spy and cause confusion.

In the military you never know when you may be put in an impossible situation. And, at those times, having strong allies may be the only way you survive. Make friends and help them often. Then call in favors whenever you need them.

Terror

In 1 Samuel 17:50-51, David incites terror in his enemies by his quick, violent actions against Goliath.

So, how did David cause terror among the Philistines?

Consider what the Philistine soldiers may have seen from a distance: On their side of the battle line, Goliath stood in magnificent armor; on the other side, a boy stood with a shepherd staff. After shouting to one another, David runs toward Goliath. And suddenly the Philistine juggernaut fell.

The use of the slingshot might have been so quick, and so unexpected, the Philistines may not have noticed it at all—expecting a champion battle with swords clashing against one another. Instead the Philistines only saw their giant—barely off their battle line—topple over.

From their perspective, many of the Philistines may have been completely unsure what happened. All they knew was their giant suddenly collapsed. As they attempt to grasp why their champion fell, David sprinted forward, drew Goliath's own sword—cutting off his head.

This inspired terror in the Philistine army. It looked like Goliath was knocked over by an unseen God—being felled without the use of a sword. Fearing they could also fall at the will of the unseen God, they flee the battlefield.

So, how can you make your enemy terrified of you?

Hit him in ways he does not expect.

Use weapons he does not expect you to use.

Use distance to your advantage.

By using a slingshot, David nullified the strength of Goliath. In the infantry this is called "weapon standoff." In other words, if your weapon range is further than your enemy's you can hit him before he can hit you. In Goliath's case, his sword could not reach as far as David's sling. So, regardless of his melee power, David's ranged attack was superior.

Pile on your attacks. When you strike your enemy, continue striking him until he is destroyed or surrenders. David did not simply hit Goliath with a stone. He ran up and beheaded him in a flash. When you strike your enemy, use violent force.

Looking further in the Bible, we see David's battlefield successes were the result of his ability to inspire terror in his enemies.

In 1 Samuel 18:12-15, 29 it says King Saul was afraid of David. As David's success continued, Saul became increasingly more intimidated by David. He suspected David would kill him and his family one day in order to take over the kingdom (1 Sam. 20:30-31). Fearing this outcome, Saul ever sought to kill David.

In 1 Samuel 19:8, David's army strikes the Philistines so violently they flee in terror.

In 1 Samuel 30:17, David and his 400 soldiers fight the Amalekite army throughout one night and day. At the end of the fighting, the remaining Amalekites fled on camels.

In 2 Samuel 5:19-20, David prays and God directs him to attack the Philistine army at Baal Perazim. Following this battle, God gives David specific instructions on how to successfully attack the Philistines in the Valley of Rephaim (2 Sam. 5:22-24). In both these battles, David inspires terror in his enemies—causing them to flee the battlefield.

In 2 Samuel 10:18, David's army caused the Arameans to flee the battlefield.

Prevent Enemy Escape

As a disclaimer, as much as possible, stop your enemy from fleeing. You do not want your enemy to get away, where he will likely rally and plan another attack. Stop him from fighting another day. Trap him on the battlefield so he cannot escape.

As you go into battle, think ahead. If your enemy were to flee from the battlefield, what direction would he travel?

By anticipating your enemy's line of retreat, you can plan accordingly—setting a follow-on ambush on their likely line of retreat. This will allow you to further exploit your enemy after a successful battle—taking full advantage of a fleeting window, turning a single battlefield victory into a decisive victory.

If you take enemy captives look over their weapons, ammo and provisions. A surrendering enemy should have ammo with him when he surrenders to you. This means he legitimately surrendered. However, if the enemy does not have ammo, this means he shot every round at you, trying to kill you—and only after he was unsuccessful he surrendered. Never trust a surrendering enemy without ammo.

Tribute Payments

The purpose of requiring tribute payments from defeated regions is to economically deprive them of the ability to once again amass sufficient military power. In the ancient world this was a common practice which allowed victorious nations to maintain control—and as their economies grew stronger, their enemies grew weaker.

In 2 Samuel 8:2, David defeats the Moabite army. He orders them to be executed, but allows some of them to live in exchange for them paying tribute to him.

In 2 Samuel 8:6, David compels the Arameans to pay tribute after defeating them in battle.

Then, in 2 Samuel 12:31, David placed garrisons within Ammonite territory after capturing the city, Rabbah. In these garrisons, David's army supervised labor within Ammonite settlements.

Tribute requirements were effective at preventing future battles as defeated nations were reduced to servitude. It was a harsh practice, but it saved the lives of countless soldiers.

Trust & Confidence

In 2 Samuel 19:5-7, David is grieving after the death of his son, Absalom. David's general Joab advantageously threatens David he will lead away the army from his kingship unless he stops grieving. David complies with Joab and stops grieving—taking his seat before his victorious army.

David overlooks Joab's threat rather than punishing him for it. He simply relieves Joab of his command by replacing him with Amasa (2 Sam. 19:13).

"Commanders intent" is a military term which means the overarching plan of your commander. This is important because in order for a subordinate leader to make the best battlefield decisions he must understand what his commander truly desires. In your military studies, make effort to understand this concept.

"Trust and confidence" must be maintained between a commander and his subordinate leaders. If at any time a commander feels as if a subordinate is not operating within his intent, the commander must relieve the subordinate. It is his prerogative on how to do this, but he cannot allow someone who is deviating from his plan to continue leading others in his unit. By allowing that subordinate to remain in place it undermines his command. Therefore, when officers and senior staff NCOs are fired, the reason cited is often "loss of trust and confidence."

In other words, subordinate leaders should be reflections of their bosses—doing their jobs the way their own bosses would do them. In order to maintain this level of trust and confidence, leaders and their subordinates must maintain professionalism and standardize behavior.

Remember, your subordinates are a direct reflection of you. Their successes are your successes. Their failures are your failures. You can delegate accountability, but you can never delegate responsibility. You are completely responsible for everything which happens in your command. Therefore you must be swift to maintain control— even by relieving subordinate leaders, if necessary.

Vigilance & Wariness

Throughout his early experiences and close calls with Saul and other enemies, David developed hypervigilance. His many narrow brushes with death taught David to constantly suspect traps. David was nearly captured by Saul many times. Moreover, he was captured by the Philistines and brought before King Achish of Gath.

David's PTSD hypervigilance is further evident in his extreme social impairment. Throughout his many psalms, David constantly suspects people of plotting against him. Although this results in him being uncomfortable around people, it protects him from many potential dangers which otherwise would have befallen him.

In 1 Samuel 23:7-12, David suspects he may be trapped within the gated city of Keilah. Thus, David's PTSD hypervigilance delivers him from capture by Saul.

In 1 Samuel 22:5, Gad the prophet warns David not to stay in the Moabite stronghold. This indicates David expected something to go awry, and he quickly moved to avoid it.

In 2 Samuel 15:27-28, David told his officials he would stay at a certain location to await messengers. Yet, even in this plan, David did not state a specific location where he might be trapped. He stated he would be in the fords of the wilderness, but he did not say exactly where.

In 2 Samuel 17:8-9 it was suspected David would be hiding somewhere separate from his troops due to him being wary of traps.

If you happen to be hypervigilant, this will work to your advantage in the military. Be wary of traps. Think about the motives of people around you. By doing this you will safeguard yourself against many ills. Do not allow yourself to become an unwitting victim. In your daily activities during deployment, you should be playing a constant game of mental chess with all the pieces around you.

All people will betray you if they are sufficiently enticed. Expect this and remain one step ahead of potential enemies at all times.

Your life depends upon your wariness and vigilance.

<u>Violence & Intensity</u>

Violence

In battle, one should ever seek to be "violent in action." When moving against one's enemies, an army should hit hard and fast. This allows an army to shift momentum in their favor as they off-balance the enemy. This forces the enemy to take a defensive posture—compelling him to either flee or continue to be pummeled.

David often uses this "violence of action" as a commander. At first he demonstrated his intensity in the champion battle against Goliath. He pressed the attack forcefully by rushing to the fallen Goliath, beheading him before his fellow soldiers could even process what happened. The result was terror.

To be most successful on battlefields, an army must move upon their enemy with intensity, violently shifting the momentum of the battle in their favor.

The enemy must be off-balanced and forced to react. Before the enemy can react to the first action, the attack must be pushed further, with violence of action, so the enemy is overwhelmed and altogether incapable of responding.

Thus, intensity and violence of action can rapidly bring an enemy to their culminating point— compelling surrender, flight or defeat.

Hit hard and fast. Keep hitting until there is nothing left, pummeling your enemy, forcing him to turtle up. Then keep pummeling him. This is "violence of action."

We see the violence of David's army in many Bible passages . . .

In 1 Samuel 19:8, David's army strikes the Philistines with such intense force they flee in terror.

In 1 Samuel 23:5, David inflicts "heavy losses" on the Philistines at Keilah. The heavy losses show the violent intensity with which David's army struck their enemies.

In 1 Samuel 30:17, David and his 400 soldiers fight the Amalekite army for one night and day. At the end of the fighting, the remaining Amalekites fled on camels.

In 2 Samuel 8:4, 13; 10:18, David had decisive victories where his army defeated thousands of enemy soldiers.

In 2 Samuel 12:29, after Joab and the army cut off the water supply in the siege of Rabbah, David gathers the remaining forces/people to make a final rush on the city. In other words, David finally commits the reserve troops to the battle, using their fresh strength to push within the city. Thus, David used fresh reserve forces in an intense action to compel immediate surrender.

In 2 Samuel 17:8 it is stated David and his men were as fierce as wild bears robbed of their cubs.

Last, in 2 Samuel 20:6, David predicts Sheba would lead his rebellion to a strong defensive position if left unchallenged. So, David sends Judah's army under the command of Abishai to pursue Sheba. The pursuit immediately put Sheba in a defensive position where he was most vulnerable.

Intensity & Threats

Often a warrior can gain a psychological advantage over an opponent through intensity—thereby preventing combat through sheer intimidation. Be willing to fight and hit your enemy hard. Make it clear, announce it, and an enemy may seek terms of peace before the battle can begin.

Notably, in 1 Samuel 25:13, 21-22, David responds with intensity against the insults of Nabal. An effective military leader should be capable of intensity—which inspires those who follow him. This intensity can be used effectively as a deterrent to battle. In this case, David's willingness to go to war immediately, and his reputation for doing so, inspired the quick action of Abigail to assuage David's offense.

Be mindful of situations where it is wise to use violent, intense speech to intimidate your enemy. Battles can be won by words before they begin. You want your presence to strike terror into the hearts of your enemies, and by doing so they will be dissuaded from doing anything to provoke you.

As a leader you want your unit to appear unassailable. If done properly, your enemy will leave you alone—preferring rather to fight against a "soft target."

Also be capable of battlefield intensity through weapon proficiency and speed. When you fight, your performance must be legendary. This will dissuade other enemy units from attempting to engage you in combat.

You must use threats sparingly so they do not lost their effect. When you threaten something, you must bear with it a reputation of following through. Otherwise your threat will be perceived as being empty.

In other words, David's threat against Nabal was effective because David had a reputation of violence. So, if you intend to use threats to psychologically manipulate your adversaries, you must have a reputation of follow-through to truly inspire fear.

War-Gaming, Contingencies & Back-up Plans

"What will you do if . . ."

A successful leader has a plan for multiple possible contingencies at all times. Battlefields are fluid environments where the only constant is "change." In war, everything is perpetually in a state of flux. As soon as one crosses the line of departure, things change. To prevent themselves from being caught off guard, warriors need to plan for contingencies.

Perhaps the best way to develop this skill is through the use of a sand table. Set up a sand table with terrain features similar to those you will encounter on your mission. Then run scenarios where the enemy does different things. Have your team leaders respond in real time to the enemy actions. Put various team members in charge of scenarios. Evaluate how they respond to each scenario—offering feedback.

Although David developed this skill as a result of his PTSD "hypervigilance," it is possible for warriors without PTSD to develop this skill through war-gaming different scenarios.

For example, in 1 Samuel 20:12-13, David and Jonathan "wargame" the two potential outcomes of Jonathan's discussion with Saul. This allowed them to mentally prepare for different outcomes—keeping them one step ahead.

As a military leader you want back-up plans for everything.

<u>Warrior</u>

In 1 Samuel 16:18, David is called a "warrior" before he is able to fight his first battle. This may seem premature, however in my opinion calling one a "warrior" speaks to his preparation for battle. Calling one a "warrior" means he is disciplined, fit and prepared for battle.

In 2 Samuel 17:10 it is stated David and his men had a reputation for their bravery and valor—noting their skill on battlefields.

If you serve in the military, embrace your call as a warrior for your nation. Focus on the development of soldierly virtues within yourself. Be a warrior.

Watchmen

In 2 Samuel 18:24-27, we see David would use watchmen within his army headquarters. Apparently they were much more observant than the watchmen of Saul—who were permitted to fall asleep (1 Sam. 26:12). David's roaming presence within his camp would have inspired watchmen and other soldiers to remain attentive to their assigned tasks.

If you are a military leader, ensure your watch-standers are disciplined. Roam around their posts unannounced and regularly check in on them to ensure they are following the orders of their assigned post.

Typically, the practice of leaders is to assign junior service-members to the late watches of the evening and early morning.

So, expect those on the latest shifts to be lax. Stop by unannounced often to keep them on their toes. Have them report their post. Ask questions and ensure they are performing their assigned duties properly throughout their entire watch.

<u>Weapon Proficiency</u>

In 1 Samuel 17:49, David kills Goliath with a slingshot. This shows David was incredibly proficient with his weapon. Doubtlessly, he spent many hours practicing the use of his slingshot. It is likely David did this while watching over his sheep in the wilderness.

Weapon proficiency is a basic requirement for all warriors. In the U.S. Marines, young warriors are told they must master their weapon—so completely their knowledge would rival the engineer who designed it.

Indeed, weapons should be revered and cherished as extensions of the warrior himself. This thought is captured in the <u>Rifleman's Creed</u>. Often the successful military unit is the one with more accurate shots. And to develop this level of weapon proficiency takes practice.

Warriors must also be familiar with the weapons of their enemies. Opportunity may demand a warrior to use his enemy's weapon.

In 1 Samuel 21:8-9, David wields the sword of Goliath—which was likely a scimitar. This demonstrates David was proficient with different kinds of swords. Likewise, military warriors should seek opportunities to grow in their knowledge of all weapons in the case where they may be required to use one of them.

Wills & Dying Wishes

In 1 Samuel 20:14-15, Jonathan makes David promise to remain kind to his family. Later, David keeps his promise to Jonathan by caring for his crippled son, Mephibosheth, after Jonathan is deceased (2 Sam. 9:7).

Never knowing who may fall on the battlefield, it is important for a military unit to ensure the will of the deceased is honored. At times a will may not be written, but spoken. Nevertheless it should be honored.

Women

It is often remarked it is impossible for women to figure out men, and it is impossible for men to figure out women. Perhaps this is why it is best to keep men at war separate from women—as they will likely encounter problems.

In the life of David, we see women are at times connected to his problems. . . .

In 1 Samuel 18:18-26, King Saul promises two marriages to David, only to later withdraw the women from him.

In 1 Samuel 21:5, David indicates women are always kept from his soldiers when they are on a mission.

In 2 Samuel 13:1-20, one of David's sons raped his half-sister. David was angry, but he failed to punish the rapist.

In 2 Samuel 11:2-5, David messes up by being involved with Bathsheba, the wife of Uriah. The story here contains several points worth mentioning. . . .

First, David should not have been gawking at another man's wife—allowing himself to lust.

Second, 2 Samuel 11:4 presents a problem if it is referring to Bathsheba cleansing herself from her monthly period. If this is the case, it is unlikely the baby could have been conceived by this one encounter between David and Bathsheba due to her ovulation cycle. If Bathsheba were purifying herself from her monthly cycle that ended on the day David saw her bathing, and if they only had intercourse on that day, it is unlikely she would have conceived (2 Sam. 11:4).

Consider, if David and Bathsheba only had sex once, on the last day of Bathsheba's period after she was purified, an egg would not have been present (2 Sam. 11:4). In this case, where only one sexual encounter is presumed, it is far more likely Bathsheba became pregnant later—perhaps with another man. If this is the case it may mean David was duped into thinking the baby was his, when it wasn't.

Another possibility: David and Bathsheba had sex multiple times following this first occasion—with Bathsheba becoming pregnant when her ovulation cycle made it possible, at least several days after the end of her period. Bathsheba would not have been capable of knowing she was pregnant until at least one month later—when she presumably would not have received her period.

Thus, a simple understanding of the ovulation cycle indicates the highest likelihood was David and Bathsheba had an ongoing affair that lasted at least one month, or that the baby was not David's.

Either way, there is more to the story.

However, we can know for certain David made a major mistake by messing with a married woman. As a result he found himself in a most bizarre situation—where he later orchestrated events to ensure the death of Bathsheba's husband, Uriah.

Overall, many of David's problems with women were results of his well-documented PTSD social impairment as found throughout his psalms. David joined the army as a young boy, immediately after defeating Goliath in a champion battle. This means David never had opportunity for normal childhood experiences—such as learning to court a woman properly. So, although he later won for himself several wives, it is no wonder why he made such large mistakes with Bathsheba. Frankly, David was not practiced in the art of properly relating to women.

Does the above discussion seem uncomfortable or tiresome to you?

I include it to illustrate a point . . .

In the military any time you allow for the mingling of men and women, you should plan to encounter problems of divers sort. And you, as the leader, will be tasked to sort out all manner of relationship problems—overseeing all potential issues which can occur between women and men. You may not know certain things, but your leadership over young men and women will require you to understand *all* these things and to be apt for teaching and prosecution.

So, be prepared for these things. Young people are involved in all manner of sexual things, and a leader needs to be familiar with what is happening so they can exercise proper leadership.

So, being a leader over young men and women requires you to understand sexual interactions—whether it makes you uncomfortable or not.

You might not feel comfortable talking to your troops about using condoms, birth control, sexual consent and so on. Get over it. You must do this.

To be a good leader you need to understand the perspectives of those you lead—which means you will need to be the one who tells them right from wrong. Frankly, if you do not instruct your troops they will make mistakes which will cost them. And, you will be dragged into problems if you do not take measures to properly counsel your troops on good behavior. Guaranteed.

So, talk to your young troops about their relationships, ensuring they are making good decisions.

Wisdom from Women

The Bible also shows us the valued wisdom of women in the life of David as well. . . .

In 1 Samuel 25:23-31, Abigail is a source of wisdom—dissuading David from attacking Nabal.

Later another wise woman dissuades Joab from attacking the town of Abel in pursuit of a traitor, named Sheba (2 Sam. 20:15-22).

Perhaps women were sources of wisdom due to their separation from battle. In other words, they could observe actions from a neutral perspective, offering wisdom to warriors like David and Joab.

For warriors like David with social impairment, it was best to avoid women altogether due to the possibility of distraction (1 Sam. 21:5). However, when women were involved in the narrative surrounding David they also presented unique, helpful perspectives which were especially enlightening.

Do not discount the unique contributions which can be offered by those who are different from you. People's differences can lend them helpful perspectives.

Genesis Pilgrim

☺